Essentials of
Teaching Academic
Oral Communication

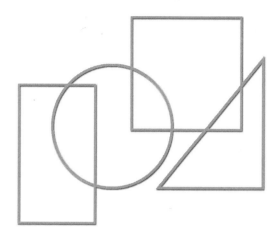

Essentials of Teaching Academic Oral Communication

ENGLISH FOR ACADEMIC SUCCESS

John Murphy
Georgia State University

SERIES EDITORS

Patricia Byrd
Joy M. Reid
Cynthia M. Schuemann

THOMSON
™
HEINLE

Australia • Canada • Mexico • Singapore • Spain • United Kingdom • United States

Essentials of Teaching Academic Oral Communication
English for Academic Success
John Murphy

Publisher: Patricia A. Coryell
Director of ESL Publishing: Susan Maguire
Senior Development Editor: Kathleen Sands-Boehmer
Editorial Assistant: Evangeline Bermas
Senior Project Editor: Kathryn Dinovo
Director of Manufacturing: Priscilla Manchester
Senior Marketing Manager: Annamarie Rice
Marketing Assistant: Andrew Whitacre

Cover graphics: LMA Communications, Natick, Massachusetts

For permission to use material from this text or product, submit a request online at http://www.thomsonrights.com

Any additional questions about permissions can be submitted by email to thomsonrights@thomson.com

Library of Congress Control Number: 2005925921

ISBN 13: 978-0-618-22492-0
ISBN 10: 0-618-22492-0

Printed in the United States of America.
23456789-EUH-10 09 08 07

For more information contact Thomson Heinle,
25 Thomson Place, Boston, MA 02210 USA, or
visit our Internet site at elt.heinle.com

Contents

Additional resources available at: www.college.hmco.com/esl/instructors

Preface

Patricia Byrd, Joy M. Reid, Cynthia M. Schuemann

The *English for Academic Success* series is a comprehensive program of student and instructor materials. For students, the series contains four levels of student language proficiency textbooks in three skill areas (oral communication, reading, and writing), with supplemental vocabulary textbooks at each level. For instructors and students, the series includes websites that support classroom teaching and learning. For instructors, four *Essentials of Teaching Academic Language* books, one for each skill area, provide helpful information for teachers new to teaching or new to teaching a particular area for academic preparation. The four books in the Essentials series are

- Coxhead, A. (2006). *Essentials of Teaching Academic Vocabulary*.
- Murphy, J. (2006). *Essentials of Teaching Academic Oral Communication*.
- Reid, J. (2006). *Essentials of Teaching Academic Writing*.
- Seymour, S., & Walsh, L. (2006). *Essentials of Teaching Academic Reading*.

Purposes of the EAS Series

The fundamental purpose of the EAS series is to prepare students who are not native speakers of English for academic success in U.S. college degree programs. By studying these materials, students in college English for academic purposes (EAP) courses will gain the academic language skills they need to be successful in degree programs. Additionally, students will learn about effective strategies for participating in U.S. college courses.

The series is based on considerable prior research as well as our own investigations of students' needs and interests, teachers' needs and desires, and institutional expectations and requirements. For example, our survey research revealed what problems teachers think they face in their classrooms, what teachers actually teach; who the students are and what they know and do not know about the "culture" of U.S. colleges; and what types of "barrier exams" are required for admission at various colleges.

In addition to meeting student needs, the EAS textbooks were created for easy implementation by teachers. First, because the books were written by experienced ESL teachers, each textbook provides instructors with a range of practical support. Second, each textbook author worked with advisory groups made up of other classroom teachers, including adjuncts as well as full-time instructors. In addition to reviewing the various drafts of the chapters, the advisory group members field-tested the materials with their own students to find out how the materials worked in class and to get student feedback for revisions. This team effort led to the development of authentic, effective, and appropriate materials that are easy to understand and to teach. Additionally, each book has an author-written website that contains helpful notes about teaching each chapter, an answer key, additional quizzes and other appropriate assessment tools, and handout and overhead masters that can be printed for use in class.

The authors and editors were also aware that many instructors find themselves teaching courses in areas that are new to them or that may not be familiar to them. To help teachers in teaching the areas covered by the EAS textbooks, a series of accompanying teacher reference books present the *essentials* of teaching academic writing, academic reading, academic oral communication, and academic vocabulary. Written by scholar-teachers, these brief, well-organized *Essentials* books provide teachers with highly focused help in developing their own knowledge and teaching skills.

Essentials Authors

As can be seen from the following summaries of their work, the authors of the *Essentials* books are true scholar-teachers who bring considerable knowledge of the classroom to their discussion of the teaching issues involved in English for academic purposes.

Averil Coxhead is the creator of the Academic Word List (AWL) that is widely used around the world as a basic tool in the development of student academic vocabulary. Now a faculty member in the School of Language Studies at Massey University in Palmerston North, New Zealand, Averil is an experienced classroom teacher of ESL, particularly of English for academic purposes, as well as a researcher on issues in second language vocabulary development.

John Murphy is a professor in the Department of Applied Linguistics & ESL at Georgia State University in Atlanta. In addition to his work with teachers in training, John has published numerous articles, both theoretical and practical, on issues in the teaching of oral communication. His highly practical strategies for teaching word syllable and stress analysis as a part of the vocabulary learning process are put into practice in the vocabulary and the oral communication textbooks in the EAS series.

Joy Reid, former president of TESOL and now retired from the University of Wyoming, is currently teaching writing in the Foundations Unit at Maui Community College in Kahului, Hawaii. Joy's work on ESL writing is recognized internationally. In addition to her publications on the theory of second language writing, she is the author and editor of many ESL composition textbooks. She brings to the task of writing her *Essentials of Teaching Academic Writing* forty years of teaching experience, as well as the publication of ESL writing textbooks and resource books for teachers.

Sharon Seymour is chair of the ESL Department at City College of San Francisco, one of the largest ESL programs in the world. In addition to her work as an administrator, she is an experienced classroom teacher. While on sabbatical in 1997, Sharon studied the reading demands of courses often taken by ESL students at her college. Using the information from that study and from other published work on academic reading, she worked with her department faculty to revise their curriculum to better prepare students to be effective academic readers. Her colleague Laura Walsh is an experienced classroom teacher who has studied the literature on second language reading and writing both as part of her graduate study and as subsequent professional development. As credit ESL assessment coordinator at City College, Laura coordinates the development, implementation, and validation of ESL placement and promotion tests. She played a primary role in revising the academic ESL curriculum. Together, these two authors bring to their *Essentials of Teaching Academic Reading* substantial knowledge of classroom teaching, of the needs of college students, and of strategies and activities for teaching academic reading.

Part **1**

Starting Off Right

Chapter **1**

Before the Course Begins

You have accepted a position to teach an oral communication course in an English-for-academic-purposes (EAP) program. You have been told that the course should develop students' listening-to-learn and speaking-to-learn abilities. Thus, you will be preparing them for college study. By the end of the program's highest-level oral communication course, students should be ready to participate as listeners and speakers in mainstream academic settings. Where should you begin?

First, assess the strengths you bring to this EAP-focused position. Realize that this is an exciting teaching opportunity. You are going to make a real difference in the lives of an interesting group of learners. You have been trained as a language teacher. You have a wealth of knowledge and skills to share with your class. You are already aware of the underlying principles of second language learning and teaching. You have considerable experience as a language teacher or teacher-in-training even if it has been in a different setting or in a different language skill. As the person in charge of the course, where should you begin? What materials should you use? What will learners expect of you and of the course?

This is also an appropriate time to take stock of who you are as a classroom teacher. All of us have beliefs, values, and presuppositions about teaching. We differ in our awareness of what some of these beliefs, values, and presuppositions might be. For example, do you tend to be a controlling presence in the classroom? Do you need to be the one clearly in charge? Can you step off center stage? Are you open to input from students? Are you flexible when your plans go awry? These are just a few questions to consider as you plan for the course. All of us have self-images as language teachers, and it is helpful to clarify for ourselves what our self-image might be.

These are the questions we all face the first time we teach a new course. Be assured, such questions never go away. They are part of the normal process of language teaching and of continued growth as a professional. As a way of finding answers to such questions, I consulted twenty-four teachers who have experience offering EAP oral communication courses. I asked them, what is the least you need to know about teaching EAP oral communication, especially when you are working with second language learners, some of whom may have graduated from U.S. secondary schools? Their answers are the substance of this book. It features discussion of the following topics:

Part 1. Starting Off Right

- What to ask about and consider before the course begins
- How to approach and what to accomplish on the first day of class
- What strategies to use for learning students' names
- How to let students know that you value their abilities as speakers of more than one language

Part 2. Speaking-to-Learn

- Defining the teaching of English for academic purposes (EAP)
- Clarifying what speaking-to-learn abilities are
- Facing special challenges as a teacher of EAP speaking
- Helping your students improve their speaking-to-learn abilities
- Addressing students' concerns

Part 3. Native English Speakers (Instructors and Peers)

- Why it is important for students to get to know their mainstream course instructors
- How to teach students ways of getting to know their instructors and native English-speaking (NES) peers
- What strategies to teach students for interacting with instructors in class and for other academic purposes
- What strategies to teach students for learning to interact with NES classmates

Part 4. The Role of Academic Lecturing

- Lectures and their pivotal role in the teaching of EAP speaking and listening
- Live lectures as central to the teaching process
- Options when preparing to present mini-lectures
- Strategies for lecturing live to the class
- Guidelines on developing lectures and lecture supports
- Lecture transcripts and video recordings
- Questions and their use in whole-class settings
- Approaches to preparing students for different class sizes and room configurations in mainstream settings

Part 5. Students' Speaking and Developing Speaking-to-Learn Abilities

- Preparing students to give oral presentations in class
- Setting up cooperative learning formats
- Arranging for students to work in dyads
- Evaluating assessment options and the role of portfolio assessment
- Introducing students to options for listening to themselves speaking English
- Teaching students how to extend the length of their speaking turns

Part 6. Vocabulary and Speech Intelligibility

- The role and importance of specialized vocabulary
- Ways of improving speech intelligibility
- Ways to help ensure the clarity of learners' speech
- Attention to word-level stress of polysyllabic words
- Accessible practice with vowel sounds of primary stressed syllables
- Attention to final consonants and word endings for purposes of speech intelligibility

Part 7. Ongoing Professional Concerns

- Adopting the stance of an exploratory teacher
- Taking seriously and learning to manipulate classroom dynamics
- Learning to work as a team player in language programs
- Locating resources: where to go to learn more

Get to Know Your Local Setting

No one wants to have to reinvent the wheel, and teachers must know enough about the program in which they will be teaching for everyone to succeed. So, here are some questions to ask—and topics to consider—that can provide essential information to help you start off well in the course.

What Does the Program Already Provide?

Do any written materials about the program describe the students, the context of the program, the program philosophy, or any other background information? Try to find an overall program manual or curriculum guide that discusses such things as the expectations of teachers, administrators, and/or students. In this era of electronic communication, most language programs post some sort of program description on the Internet for student recruitment purposes. Whatever information you can find about the program (e.g., its local environment, its special characteristics, kinds of students who attend), these are essential places to begin.

Make the most of opportunities to get to know the players you will be working with. Take advantage of opportunities to get to know such key personnel as the program director, other administrators, and teachers. Also meet potential students, staff personnel, AV support personnel, library contacts, and so forth. As you meet these various people, keep the following in mind:

1. Prepare yourself to be perceived as a professional. Develop a reputation of excellence and collegiality within the program. Everyone wants to work with capable colleagues. Part of your role should be to develop constructive working relationships with as many of the people you will be working with and meeting as you can. Be creative in ensuring that you are helpful and supportive not only of your students' efforts but of your supervisors' and colleagues' efforts as well.

2. Be sensitive to the college's budgetary constraints and the level of support staff personnel. For example, if there is just one overworked secretary (more commonly known as an administrative assistant), it would be unwise to expect this person to have the time to answer all your questions. Also, most programs have only one or a few administrative assistants, and they are rarely available to perform such tasks as to type or to photocopy materials for teachers.

3. Find out the program's expectations in terms of teachers' office hours, attendance at meetings, teacher absences, participation on committees, and the like. Whatever the program's expectations, work not only to meet them but to surpass them. This does not mean, for example, that you must have more office hours than is expected for other teachers. Some ways to go the extra mile are to clearly feature your office hours, office telephone number, and e-mail address in your course syllabus for students to see. As you get to know the students, speak with them about the importance of taking advantage of office hours. Make yourself readily available, and be sure the office staff are aware of your office hours. Encourage the staff to put a student in contact with you whenever they receive telephone queries about your availability. Similar ways of going the extra mile apply to your participation in program meetings, committee work, and virtually all interactions with colleagues and supervisors.

4. Although I list numerous questions here, take stock of the program's environment on your own. It is fine to ask questions of administrative assistants and colleagues, but some answers may be found in policies and procedures materials. You do not want to give an initial impression of being a pest. Read through any printed materials or manuals, and save your questions for items not addressed in such resources.

5. How are book orders placed? Who selects the book(s) to be used in the course you will teach? Has a textbook already been ordered for the course? How can you secure a copy, preferably a "desk copy"? Around the time that books are to arrive in the bookstore, visit the facility. Get to know bookstore personnel. Make it part of your role to track when the text will be available for purchase.

6. At what point at the start of the semester will you be expected to submit a course syllabus (or curriculum plan)? Are models or illustrations already available that you could review in preparation?

7. For the EAP oral communication course you will be teaching, ask yourself (and others) the following: What should learners be able to do by the end of the course if they have participated in it successfully? What particular EAP speaking-to-learn and listening-to-learn abilities should successful students have mastered? Talk with other teachers, and review professional literature (Internet resources, books, journal articles) to learn more about EAP oral communication needs.

8. Who develops the curriculum and course objectives? Are these already established within the program, or are you responsible for setting them and/or modifying them?

9. What degree of photocopying support is available? How do you gain access to the facilities? What procedures must you follow for using the photocopier? When are good times to use the machine? Who can lend assistance when the machine fails to function properly? Office personnel commonly are busy with other matters. Learn to run the photocopiers and other machines so that you can work out kinks on your own. Always be reasonable in your expectations of support from others.

10. What other equipment and materials are available (e.g., audiovisual equipment, tape and CD players, video support, computer classrooms, a system of student e-mail, language laboratories, a tutoring center), and what are the procedures for obtaining access to such support?

11. Does the program expect the course to be connected with a course Internet site?

12. What are the program's procedures on grading policies or other forms of assessment that must be incorporated into the course?

13. In addition to regular grades, are you expected to submit anything along the lines of interim student progress reports, prose assessments of students' projects, or samples of students' work? If so, when must such materials be made available and in what format? Be sure to follow through on your supervisors' expectations in these and similar areas.

14. When and how are students provided opportunities to complete evaluation-of-faculty reports? Does this happen just at the end of the course, or are multiple opportunities provided for formative feedback throughout the course?

15. While gathering information on procedural and scholastic matters, be sure to attend any orientation meetings arranged by the program. Develop even more sustained contacts with other teachers in the program. Reach out to teachers who may have already taught the course you will be teaching and to those who may be teaching alternative levels (or sections) of the same or similar course(s). Spend some time with them (e.g., a lunch or coffee date). Ask if they would share sample course syllabi and other instructional materials with you. Also contact teachers who teach other language skills and abilities (e.g., writing or reading for academic purposes, grammar). When you do, gather as much information as possible about other courses, as well as about the program's overall structure, instructional philosophy, and content focus.

16. Ask about such practical matters as whether telephone and e-mail listings are available for teachers and the office staff. Clarify what will be expected of you as the course instructor; learn as much as you can from others who work in the program. Even if you are an experienced teacher, when you are new to a program there is always a lot to learn about local realities. Here are additional questions to consider and to try to find additional information about:

    - What is the teaching philosophy of the program overall?
    - What styles of teaching are valued?
    - Are any teaching styles frowned upon?

- How are such styles as teacher-fronted instruction, technology-mediated teaching, or frequent use of group work perceived by administrators and colleagues?
- What is the teaching philosophy for this particular course?
- How has the course been offered in the past?
- Which facets of spoken communication are usually emphasized?
- Have any problems come up in the past? (Usually they have.)
- What course features have worked well? What features have been problematic?
- Which key people can help you set up a plan for the course?
- Is there anything like an MA TESOL teacher training program in the area? If there is, you might be able to solicit degree candidates as tutors or in-class teacher aides. If such possibilities are available, keep your program director well informed. It is essential that she or he support any initiatives you may take along these lines.
- What textbooks have been used? Which ones were better received by learners?

Also be sure to learn about such practical matters as:

- Has a classroom for your course already been assigned?
- What are the classrooms like?
- Where are they located?
- Are the rooms large/small, noisy/quiet?
- Is any construction going on in the area? If so, will it affect the quality of the classroom environment?
- Are classrooms adequately heated in the winter and cooled in the summer? Sometimes nothing can be done about such matters, but at least you would be able to advise students and dress accordingly. If appropriate, seek alternative rooms and submit a room request through the normal channels.
- Do the rooms or other facilities have any problems you should know about?
- What types of technological support are available (e.g., chalkboard, VCR players, audio players, Internet connection, Power Point display)?
- What resources are available in the library or resource center (e.g., computers, software, audio and video recordings, newspapers, magazines)?

Visit the Classroom

A few days prior to the start of the course, visit the classroom you will be using. Find a time when the room is empty. Check things out. See how the light switches, windows, shades, and so forth operate. Are the students' seats moveable or located in fixed positions? How does the overhead projection and VCR/DVD equipment operate? Is there a central instructor's technology station? Look up and make a note of telephone numbers for personnel who can support your use of the room's electronic equipment. If you have doubts about the use of the equipment, contact these persons. Write on the display board. Does it use chalk, or some sort of marker? What type of marker, if any, should not be used on the display board? What supplies will you need to request or carry with you in order to teach?

While in the classroom, listen to yourself while speaking aloud. Vary the projection of your voice from a whisper to incrementally louder projections. Spend a few minutes listening to your own voice and how it interfaces with the room's acoustics. Learn to make adjustments as necessary.

Is the ventilation system noisy? Do street sounds enter the room? Are there any other sources of sound that may distract students? If you notice any serious problems with the room, find out how to request a room change.

What level of office or staff support is provided to teachers or students?

- Office space
- Computers
- Internet access
- Assistance from the office staff
- Access to photocopy equipment

Spend some time getting the lay of the land. Be aware that office space may be limited. If you have to share space with colleagues, be sensitive to their needs for space, too. Especially if you are asked to share an office with other people, it is your responsibility to avoid intruding into space reserved for others. In addition to visiting your assigned classroom(s), visit offices you will be working in or sending students to, such as library facilities.

Stay in Touch with Available Resources

You may be teaching this course/subject matter for some time. It is important to be well informed on contemporary developments in the teaching of speaking and listening for academic purposes. Even if you have previously completed coursework in methods of ESL teaching, reacquaint yourself with discussions of relevant teaching methods in the more recent, widely used ESL methods texts (see reference information in the endnote at the end of this chapter).[1]

Listed not in alphabetical order but in order of importance to the teaching of academic oral communication, the following references are my top ten picks for those interested in reading more professional literature. Because most of us probably do not have copies of these readily available, request a few of the items through interlibrary loan. For example, the first two items, by Ferris and Tagg, are essential readings in this area. Murphy's (1991) useful article discusses integrated instruction in listening, speaking, and pronunciation. Mendelsohn (1991/92) is especially strong on assessment options. If you have limited time, these are four obvious places to begin.

Top Ten References for Learning More about the Teaching of Academic Oral Communication

1. Ferris, D., & Tagg, T. 1996a. Academic oral communication needs of EAP learners: What subject-matter instructors actually require. *TESOL Quarterly, 30*(1), 31–58.
2. Ferris, D., & Tagg, T. 1996b. Academic listening/speaking tasks for ESL students: Problems, suggestions, and implications. *TESOL Quarterly, 30*(2), 297–320.
3. Murphy, J. 1991. Oral communication in TESOL: Integrating speaking, listening, and pronunciation. *TESOL Quarterly, 25*(2), 51–76.
4. Mendelsohn, D. J. 1991/92. Instruments for feedback in oral communication. *TESOL Journal, 1*(2), 25–30.
5. Mendelsohn, D. 1992. Making the speaking class a real learning experience: The keys to teaching spoken English. *TESL Canada Journal, 10*(1), 72–89.
6. Bailey, K. M. & Savage, L. 1994. *New ways in teaching speaking.* Alexandria, VA: TESOL.
7. Brown, H. D. 2001. Teaching oral communication skills. In *Teaching by principles: An interactive approach to language pedagogy* (pp. 267–297). New York: Longman.
8. Chaudron, C. 1995. Academic listening. In D. J. Mendelsohn & Rubin, J. (Eds.), *A guide for the teaching of listening* (pp. 74–96). San Diego, CA: Dominie Press.
9. Flowerdew, J. 1994. *Academic listening: Research perspectives.* New York: Cambridge University Press.
10. Murphy, J. 1992. Preparing ESL students for the basic speech course: Approach, design, and procedure. *English for Specific Purposes, 11*(1), 51–70.

To continue your development as a teacher of speaking and listening for academic purposes, set for yourself the goal of reading these sources over the coming months until you are familiar with all of them. A related challenge is to integrate some of their concepts and strategies for teaching along with your own teaching styles and your ways of conceptualizing the course. Also, read recent publications and attend conference presentations that may be useful for enhancing the evolution of your course as you continue to develop it.

What Is the Existing Oral Communication Curriculum or Content of the Course?

The goals of a course in listening and speaking for academic purpose are the broad, macro level, or general goals that students should achieve by the time they finish your course. Course goals must be conceptualized and worded in reference to what students need to gain from the course. It is important to identify goals in terms of *what students should be able to do by the end of the course,* and not in terms of what you as their teacher should do or what the textbook or lessons should provide. For example, a broad course goal for the highest-level course in this area would serve as an answer to the following overarching question:

Question to help identify goals for the highest-level EAP oral communication course:

What must students be able to do as listeners and speakers in academic settings by the end of the course (i.e., during their initial years of college study) as a result of having participated in the course successfully?

Some related subquestions to consider:

1. What listening-to-learn and speaking-to-learn abilities must they have by end of the course or EAP program?
2. How may the course goals be sequenced within the program's overall oral communication curriculum?
3. What is the trajectory of course goals across the various levels of EAP oral communication courses offered by the program?

At the macro level of an overall curriculum of study, the goals of the four-level series of EAP oral communication textbooks are *to develop speaking and listening skills necessary for college study.* These goals are accomplished by providing EAP learners with direct instruction in how to handle, respond to, and contribute to the language used in college classes. EAP oral communication students must learn to participate effectively in a variety of academic situations, including discussions, lectures, debates, other in-class activities, student study groups, and office meetings with their college teachers. They also must learn to communicate with other class members and professors over the telephone and to leave and respond to concise but informative voice-mail messages. They must be able to request information from instructors and native English-speaking (NES) peers. These are large and challenging goals for EAP learners to meet. In the series, the goals are spread across four textbooks aimed at four levels of sophistication and proficiency in using English for academic purposes.

At the level of individual books tied to specific courses, think of course objectives as detailed statements about what students must be able to do to meet macro-level goals. Some examples of goals and objectives in EAP oral communication may illustrate these points.

The goals and objectives of Book 1 just scratch the surface as far as developing students' abilities in these areas; those of Book 3 and especially of Book 4 prepare students more directly for content-area college study. Book 4's focus on the preparation of listening-to-learn and speaking-to-learn abilities relevant for college study is the clearest to recognize. Books 1, 2, and 3 lay preliminary groundwork while moving students in level-appropriate EAP directions through incremental stages.

Even if you are not using the series for the course you offer, review the goals and objectives listed above. They will illustrate the kinds of course emphases that are relevant to a course sequence within an EAP oral communication curriculum. The textbook authors worded the goals and objectives in measurable terms tied to what students must be able to do by the end of the course. Part of your role as a teacher in this subject area is to teach toward these types of goals and objectives. The remaining discussion in this book will assist you along the journey.

Things to Check and Do

- Have you taken the time to assess the strengths and weaknesses you bring to this teaching opportunity?
- Have you made a list of questions you really need to find answers for?
- Have you divided your questions into two groups—those for which you can find answers on your own, and those you need to speak with others about? To establish a good first impression, take the time to find as many answers as you can on your own.
- What realistic expectations should you have from the program and the support the program can offer?
- Have you been thinking about course goals?
- Have you reviewed professional literature on course goals?
- Have you consulted with others?
- Have you asked yourself the following questions?
  - What must college students be able *to do* as a result of having been successful participants in the course?
  - What must college students be able to do as *speakers* in academic settings, both in classrooms and as part of other related course responsibilities?
  - What must college students be able to do as *listeners* in academic settings, both in classrooms and as part of other related course responsibilities?
- Have you thought about and planned for presenting yourself as a strong colleague in your interactions with others?

Endnote

1. Brown, H. D. 2001. *Teaching by principles: An interactive approach to language pedagogy.* Englewood Cliffs, NJ: Prentice Hall Regents.

Reference

Celce-Murcia, M. (Ed.). 2001. *Teaching English as a second or foreign language* (2nd ed.). Boston: Heinle & Heinle.

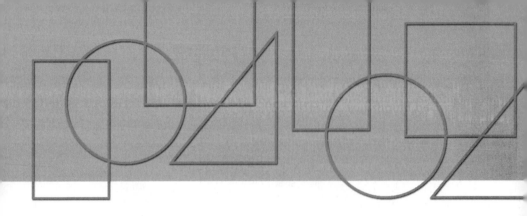

Chapter **2**

The First Day of Class

When structured well, the first day of class can be highly productive. Depending on your plans and what you are able to accomplish, it can make a large difference in setting the right tone for the rest of the term. On the first day, everything is fresh and new. Everyone is full of anticipation, students and teacher alike. You can be sure that some members of the class will be nervous about participating in a course tied to English for academic purposes (EAP) speaking and listening abilities.

SOMETHING STUDENTS NEED TO KNOW

English for academic purposes (EAP) refers to the teaching of English to speakers of other languages in college preparatory courses. EAP courses are usually offered by intensive English programs designed to prepare second language learners of English for success as college students. EAP courses provide opportunities for learners to acquire the study skills college students need in order to succeed in mainstream content area courses. Depending on local programmatic structures, ESL students enrolled in EAP courses may (or may not) also be enrolled in a few mainstream college courses at the same time.

At the start of the term, students may be anxious about getting to know you. They will want to learn more about the course. They will be wondering what kind of teacher you are: Are you competent? Are you patient? Are you fair? Are you easily flustered? Do you take students' ideas and concerns seriously? Do you enjoy teaching? At the very least, students will want to know that you can structure a useful course and that you are both a reasonable human being and a competent teacher.

A few students may resent being enrolled in a course they perceive as tangential to their ultimate academic goals. Part of your role on the first days of class is to convince them that you and the course will serve them well. A good way to address these concerns is to convey your commitment to and enthusiasm for the course. Show them that you are well prepared, that you take your role seriously, and that the course focuses on abilities they must master in order to succeed as college students. Remember, the first day of class helps set the tone for the rest of the term.

As mentioned in Chapter 1, visit the classroom long before the first day of class. Develop a feel for its physical space. Find out where the nearest rest rooms are so that you can mention their locations to the class. Spend some time writing on the chalkboard until you are accustomed to using it. Be sure your handwriting will be legible from everywhere in the room. Consider (or make a list of) the room's physical features that will be important to how you offer the course.

Set Out to Establish a Sense of Community in the Classroom

In general, students respond well when they recognize that you are doing your best to treat them politely, respectfully, and professionally. On the first days of class, everyone is a bit nervous. Minimally, students want to get to know you and their classmates. Set up activities that provide opportunities for students to meet and learn a bit about each other. Names are especially important on the first day of the class. Use activities that challenge everyone to learn each other's names. You do not have to leave the room with everyone's name on the tip of your tongue, but demonstrate that you are attempting to learn names and that you are encouraging everyone else to do the same. I will return to this topic later in this chapter.

As appropriate, try to learn something mildly personal about each class member. For example, I ask students to share information on one of the following: a favorite song, a novel, a movie, a recording artist, an actor, a poem. I also ask students to explain a favorite hobby or pastime. Write some of this information down on index cards. Distribute a blank index card to each class member, and have students write down whatever information you would like to have easily accessible.

Name
ID Number
E-mail Address
Telephone Numbers
Year of Arrival in the Unites States
Projected Major
Other Languages(s)
Something Personal (hobbies, interests)
Brief Physical Self-Description

I find that when I am able to associate something personal with each student, it is easier to remember names. Once I have collected the index cards, I use them both in and out of class as flash cards to learn names and in other ways to learn about everyone in the class.

Consider Bringing a Camera to the First Day of Class

One way to get to know students is to leave the first class session with a visual record. An Instamatic camera or a cell phone with photo capability is useful for this purpose. Given the availability of one-hour photo development stores, even a conventional camera will do. Before everyone leaves the room, ask permission to take a few snapshots of the class. Explain that you will be using the pictures to associate names with faces and that doing so will speed up the process of your getting to know the class better. Another option is to use a camcorder for similar purposes. A brief recording produced with a camcorder is especially useful if you will be using such technology as part of the course. The sooner students start to learn about the technology the better.

Introduce the Course

Students are investing considerable time, energy, and money into being members of the class. Let them know what the course is all about. Tell them you will focus on developing their "listening-to-learn" and "speaking-to-learn" abilities. Explain what you mean by such terms. Discuss some of the listening-to-learn and speaking-to-learn expectations of college classes. Remember that this is only a preliminary discussion of these central course themes. You will go into more detail in subsequent classes. However, students really want to know that the course will address their needs. They want to know what you mean by the terms *listening-to-learn* and *speaking-to-learn.*

> ### SOMETHING STUDENTS NEED TO KNOW
>
> **Listening-to-learn** refers to the kinds of listening abilities college students need in order to learn the challenging content in mainstream, academic, content area courses. One obvious listening-to-learn ability that college students need is the capacity to learn content materials while listening to and taking notes on lectures. The term **speaking-to-learn** refers to the kinds of speaking abilities college students need in order to participate interactively with professors and classmates while learning the challenging content featured in mainstream courses. For example, college students periodically need to speak up in class to ask questions of lecturers. Outside class, students need to participate as speakers in study groups with classmates while getting ready for an upcoming quiz or test. In such settings, students use speaking-to-learn behaviors.

Discuss these major themes at the start of the course, even if only briefly. Elaborate your initial explanation over the next few weeks. Students will want to know how much work will be required. Will they have to speak in public (at the front of the room with all eyes on them)? What listening and speaking tasks will be featured in the course? How will they be assessed?

Show students the textbook and any supplementary reading materials. Either distribute the syllabus and go over it with the class, or first introduce the course orally and distribute the syllabus at the end of the class. Because a sound introduction to the course is an essential part of setting the right tone for the rest of the term, I never find it a good idea to end class early on the first day. A better option is to begin to establish some patterns of classroom activities and overall tone that will be repeated throughout the term.

Establish a Comfortable Atmosphere for the Course

Especially in a course focused on oral communication, you need to set and maintain a comfortable affective environment. By arriving at the classroom a few minutes ahead of time, you will be setting a good example for students to do so on a regular basis. Talk with students as they enter the room. Begin the class on time. By doing so, you are modeling punctuality as a valued part of academic life. Likewise, finish each class on time. Your own commitment to punctuality demonstrates to students that you respect them as people and that you are aware of and respect their other campus commitments. Your model of punctuality and respect for their time also better prepares them for their eventual transitions into college-level study and the expectations of mainstream course instructors.

Encourage questions and other forms of feedback/input from all class members. It is not enough merely to say such things as "Please ask me if you have any questions." I find that when teachers use a phrase such as "Are there any questions?" most of the time their query merely cuts off rather than opens interaction with the class. Especially when the class does not know you well, you need to follow your invitations for student questions with a sufficient amount of time for someone to speak up. This deliberate pausing is called *wait time*, and teachers can lengthen their wait time in classrooms to good effect. As simple as this may seem, many teachers miss such opportunities.

Alternatively, ask students to write any questions they might have on a slip of paper. Then collect and use the written questions to generate more class dialogue. Whatever strategies you use to get to know students better, demonstrate that you are open to students' voices by your moment-to-moment behaviors as their teacher.

Students learn quickly if a teacher is insincere or if the teaching behaviors they witness fail to meet their needs for responsive teaching. Whenever possible, make yourself available by remaining in the classroom at least for a few minutes once class is over. Both during and at the end of class, avoid the tendency to look down or away from students too often. Make it a habit to maintain eye contact with at least a few members of the class. By keeping an open and solicitous expression with your eyes, face, and other dimensions of body language, you will be encouraging class members to approach you on their own. These are important opportunities to answer questions and address concerns students may be reluctant to voice during class. In addition, by remaining in the room after class, you will be in a better position to gauge how well students are responding to the course and to you as their instructor. It is often the unplanned conversations at the end of class, or the walk with a student in the hallway that gives you insight into how students are responding to the course from their perspective.

Learn about Students' Dreams and Fears

A useful way to identify students' needs while establishing a comfortable atmosphere for learning is to design a relevant classroom activity. One such activity I find especially helpful is called "Dreams and Fears." Begin the activity by asking everyone present to help you define the words *dreams* and *fears*. These are concepts that most students will be able to discuss with relative ease. Because they are familiar topics, such a discussion is a good one at the start of the course.

Once the concepts are sufficiently clear, ask students to start thinking about what they really want to get out of the course. Ask what their dreams are and what they want to accomplish as speakers of English. Whom do they want to be able to speak with? What do they want to be able to do with the spoken language? What opportunities do they want to see opened? Where do they want to be able to use their spoken English?

Also ask students to focus on what their fears are as speakers of English. In what kinds of situations do they encounter difficulties? Do they ever feel nervous or apprehensive while speaking in English? Have they ever felt reluctant to speak because they felt uncomfortable? Initially, ask students to work alone as they generate a private listing of their own dreams and fears as English speakers. After a few minutes, extend the classroom activity so that students can work in pairs or slightly larger groups to list dreams and fears collaboratively. Eventually, distribute large flip-chart-size sheets of paper (or transparency sheets) and markers. Ask each group to transfer their listings of dreams and fears to the paper.

Once everyone is ready, ask students to post their lists on the classroom walls. Provide appropriate fasteners for posting these materials around the classroom.

Did you know that magnets work well as fasteners on most modern display boards? I avoid calling them blackboards because the ones to which magnets adhere are usually green. Otherwise, another good option for fastening large sheets of paper is adhesive tape. Also, if your program has the resources, purchase classroom-size Post-it paper from office supply stores.

Ask a representative from each group to speak to the class about the dreams and fears they have been discussing. The activity is useful for several reasons. First, it is a speaking activity through which you and everyone else can hear the voices of class members. Students are having opportunities to get to know each other better. Second, as students are articulating what their dreams and fears are, you can keep track of what they say from the perspective of needs analysis. Take notes on what students say. Ask permission to save their notes and the large sheets of paper. Such classroom artifacts provide a glimpse into what students want to get out of the course. Review the information you gather to plan upcoming classroom activities and topics to introduce.

Finally, once the group representatives have completed their presentations, take a few minutes to address the entire class. While using this time to bring closure to the activity, remind students that the course will not be able to treat in detail all the topics and concerns the students have been discussing. Go over some students' examples, and use them to discuss course parameters in a realistic way. Look for examples that can be tied to EAP speaking-to-learn or listening-to-learn abilities, and expand these to help define what the course is about. The final opportunities you take to clarify course goals and objectives are perhaps the most useful phases of the "dreams and fears" activity.

Manage Your Own Anxiety

Whenever we start something new, we inevitably experience moments of uneasiness. Most of us find that teaching in general, and language teaching in particular, is an anxiety-provoking endeavor. Anxious moments are a normal part of a teacher's life, just as alternative forms of anxiety are part of a student's life. Be aware of your own moments of anxiety. If possible, do something about them. Use breathing or other relaxation exercises to relieve stress or to calm yourself. An effective way to get over anxious moments is to find a private place and alternatively tense and then relax the muscles of your shoulders, neck, and arms. By alternately tensing and relaxing the muscles, you are putting yourself in control of some physical correlates of anxiety. Take advantage of whatever tension reduction strategies are familiar to you (e.g., visualization techniques, taking a walk, yoga, tai chi, meditation, prayer, breathing exercises, stretching exercises).

One of my colleagues always sets aside fifteen minutes for private time in her office to practice breathing exercises prior to walking to her classroom. She considers this time an essential part of her preparation for an effective class.

Make Sure Everyone Is in the Right Place

One of the first things you will want to do on the first day is be sure that everyone in the room is supposed to be there. Start off by writing the name and official numbers for the course on the board. Explain briefly what the title of the course refers to, and ask the students to check their course schedules to be sure they are in the right classroom. It is very common for one or two people to have come to the wrong room. Give them an opportunity to leave the room as unobtrusively as possible.

Take Care of Any Administrative Tasks

Expect that the department will require certain administrative tasks not only on the first day of class but on many class meetings for the rest of the term. Create a file folder you can bring to class in which to place announcements you want to make. Be sure to take attendance. There are many options: call the roll sometime near the start of class, put a student in charge of taking attendance, or rotate this responsibility. I like to make it obvious when I am calling the role so that students realize they are being held accountable for attendance.

Learn Students' Names

Few things are as important to students as being sure their teacher knows who they are. Because names are an integral part of the personal sense of self, they are important to everyone. Their role is especially important in oral communication classrooms. It is essential that a teacher try to learn students' names quickly. Doing so allows more personal connections with students and can go far in easing some of the classroom management challenges all teachers face. For example, it is much easier for teachers to use questioning strategies effectively, to structure group work efficiently, and to provide feedback when needed if they can use students' names with confidence. Knowing students' names early on makes many dimensions of language teaching easier, especially classroom management dimensions.

Assess Your Strengths and Weaknesses in Learning Names

When it comes to learning and remembering new names, most people have room for improvement. If you are typical, unable to remember names easily, develop a deliberate plan that will assist you. Be focused and well organized in your attempts. Make yourself do this. It will make a clear difference in your teaching.

Ask Students to Help

Ask students to complete written profiles on the first day of class. During this initial class, have students fill in a personal identification form, something more elaborate than the index cards mentioned earlier. The form might request telephone numbers, address, major area of study, any previous EAP courses, first languages, year of arrival in the United States, employment status, name and location of secondary school, brief family history, and so on. Somewhere on the form, however, include an item such as the following:

> "Please provide a brief physical description of yourself. Tell me some things about your physical appearance that will help me remember you and learn your name more quickly."

By asking students to self-describe themselves, you will be tapping into some of their self-perceptions. Self-descriptions generated by learners are usually helpful when it comes to your remembering and learning new names. For example, a recent student took this opportunity to mention that she wears a flesh-colored hearing aid in each ear. This information made it easier for me to remember her name, and it also kept me informed about the student's special needs from the very first day of class.

Videotape the Members of Your Class

A very effective strategy for learning students' names quickly is to bring a camcorder to class on the first or second day. Without taking up too much classroom time, pan around the room with the camera to get a visual record of the class. This is a simple action and does not take much time. If you are more ambitious, point the camera at individual class members while you ask them to look into the camera and (1) say their name, (2) repeat their name a second time, and (3) say something brief about themselves (e.g., a hobby, a favorite movie, book, or TV show).

One reason I like videotaping is that I can repeatedly review the recording at home prior to the next day of class. Videos are ready immediately, no processing time required. When playing it back, place the recording on pause or slow motion from time to time. As you scan the faces on the screen, test your memory for their names. After playing the recording in these ways, I usually arrive for the second day of class already knowing everyone's name. Although there is always the concern that use of a camcorder may intimidate some students, the point is to learn names and to associate faces with names as quickly as possible. Ahead of time, I apologize to students for using the recording machine while explaining that I will be depending on it as an aid in my struggle to learn their names. In a later section of this book, I discuss other potential benefits of using camcorders in ESL courses. Introducing such technology on one of the initial days of class to learn students' names is a small step in enticing learners into using such resources for more productive purposes later in the course.

Use Index Cards as Flash Cards

Earlier, I mentioned the strategy of using index cards as flash cards, but I expand on it here. The idea is to create a set of three-by-five index cards with each student's name and some self-description on them. I hand out blank cards during the first class and ask students to write down the information I want to learn. I have them write out their full names, as well as any preferred nicknames, and ask them to place a circle around the name they prefer I use in class. Once you have collected the completed cards, carry them with you wherever you go for a few days and flip through the set during free moments. By reviewing the cards repeatedly and in a structured way, you will be getting to know the members of your class.

Ask Students to Follow the "First Letter Only" Rule

Because I want to learn their names and because I want them to realize
I am taking steps to do so as quickly as possible, I involve students in
assisting me as follows. If a student notices I am not using his name or if
he hears me say anything like, "Sorry, but I cannot remember your name,"
I ask him to tell me the first letter only of his first name. In this way, I
provide learners with opportunities to support my efforts (they give
me a first letter as a clue) but I still have to do some cognitive work to
remember full names.

Taking this step is more effective than merely having a student tell you
hers or his whole name. So if a student notices my memory lapse and then
says "*N*" or "it starts with an *N*," it is more likely that I will remember the
student is named "Nativia" on my own. Once I have first names under
control, I ask students to do the same with the first letter of their family
names. I find the "first letter rule" to be a great aid in learning the names
of the entire class.

Some students have a lot of fun with this process. When I meet
students outside the classroom—while walking across campus, for
example—they sometimes tease me by looking me straight in the eye
while saying, "It starts with a(n) ___." Along these lines, to modify the
way I use the camcorder on the first day of class, I first ask each student to
simply say the first letter of her or his first name as the preliminary piece
of information. Then each student provides the additional information.
Later, when viewing the recording in private, I challenge myself to figure
out each student's name from these initial cues.

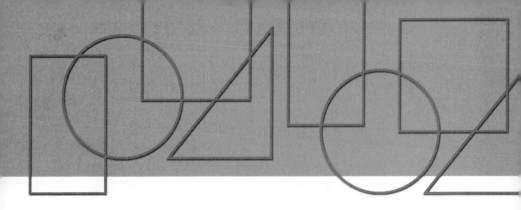

Chapter **3**

Speakers of More than One Language Are Terrific!

FEATURED IN THIS CHAPTER

- Ways of acknowledging learners' strengths
- Useful resources on language interference problems
- How to share your own background as a language learner

Most students in your course speak two or more languages. This ability places them in a select group because the great majority of college students in the United States speak only English. At the start of your course, celebrate the fact that you value your students' abilities as language learners. This chapter offers practical tips on assisting learners in feeling proud about the language abilities they already possess and bring to the course. These tips will help you in establishing healthy rapport with your students from the very first day of class.

Part **2**

Speaking-to-Learn

Chapter **4**

Special Challenges
of EAP Speaking

FEATURED IN THIS CHAPTER

- Challenges when speaking-to-learn
- The aims of this book and of your course
- Differences between spoken and written language
- Characteristics of mainstream college classrooms
- How to recognize differences between groups of learners
- Why length of residence matters

Speaking in a second language is not easy. We all want to be understood by others when we speak. In addition to making clear some distinctions between speaking for social, academic, and other purposes, it is important to discuss the process of ESL speaking in general. Speaking in a second language can be anxiety provoking, especially when learners are asked to speak in front of a large group. College classrooms are examples of such settings. Not only are at least several dozen people present, but students are challenged to speak on substantive topics that are centered on new information and challenging concepts. Under such circumstances, it is no wonder that in mainstream college settings many second language learners of English tend to depend on their native English speaking (NES) peers to do most of the interactive work with course instructors.

A common strategy ESL college students use is to listen to and monitor exchanges between the instructor and other class members without contributing very much on their own. The aims of this book and your course are to change such patterns. Your challenge is to provide requisite tools and experiences so that students in your class can participate as speakers in English-medium college classes when they feel the need or inclination to do so. That is an essential dimension of our job as EAP professionals. We need to provide the tools so that students can make informed decisions about what will become their speaking-to-learn behaviors in college classes. Of course, the degree of eventual participation in mainstream courses ultimately will be up to the students. As an EAP teacher, your responsibility is to prepare them to make appropriate decisions concerning when and if to contribute to class discussions and other speaking-to-learn opportunities from a position of confidence rather than insecurity. Students should feel confident enough and be strong enough linguistically to contribute to class discussion in English if and when they choose to do so.

Why Give Special Attention to EAP Speaking?

When expressing ourselves in a second language, we are really putting our self-images on the line. This is especially true for students talking in their second language in the relatively public forum of a college classroom. For EAP learners, the challenges of participating in class are compounded by multiple-language apprehensions, concerns about self-image, and cultural differences. As you plan for the content focus of your EAP oral communication course, keep some of the special characteristics and challenges of spoken language in mind.

Some major differences between spoken and written language forms:

Spoken Language	Written Language
▪ More ephemeral, less permanent	▪ More permanent
▪ Rate of delivery controlled by speaker, and listeners are dependent on speakers	▪ Reading rate controlled by the reader
▪ More use of colloquial language	▪ Language use more formalized
▪ Coordinated with body language	▪ Coordinated with written discourse conventions and coherence features
▪ Uses stress, rhythm and intonation as listeners' navigation guides	▪ Uses punctuation and other graphic markers as readers' navigation guides
▪ Potential for immediate listener responses	▪ Responses are distanced by space and time, no immediate interaction
▪ More personal, interpersonal	▪ More detached from the personal
▪ Uses naturally occurring redundancy	▪ Uses more complex sentence structure
▪ More coordinate clauses	▪ More subordinate clauses
▪ Uses longer phrases and sentences	▪ Uses longer words
▪ More questions and exclamations	▪ More prepositional phrases
▪ High use of "BE" verb constructions	▪ More use of passive voice
▪ More use of personal pronouns	▪ More noun phrases
▪ More reduced clauses	▪ More participial phrases
▪ Dialogic	▪ Monologic
▪ Interactive between speakers and listeners	▪ Planned by the writer

While comparing these differences between spoken and written language, keep in mind that the spoken language of college classrooms begins to manifest some characteristics of written language. These shared characteristics reflect some ways in which spoken language used for social purposes differs at times from more academic styles of spoken discourse. Whereas spoken language used for everyday social purposes tends to be tied to highly contextualized "here and now" topics, the language of academic lectures tends to be more context reduced and refers to external events and concepts.

Keep in Mind the Challenges EAP Speakers Face

Remember that you are preparing learners to be active participants in college classes beyond the ESL program. Therefore, it is imperative to keep in mind the realities of college classrooms beyond the program in which you are teaching. Consider the kinds of speaking performances expected in mainstream college classes. Certainly, students must be able to speak up during class from time to time. College students are expected to ask questions of their professors during class. They must know how to interact with college lecturers. They often are called on to participate in small-group tasks and study sessions.

Set Up Activities that Simulate the Formats of Mainstream College Classrooms

What activity types are featured most frequently in college classrooms? College instructors lecture to the whole class, set up discussion groups, and sometimes use small-group and pair activities. Occasionally, they ask students to report back to the whole class following group discussions. They may ask an individual student, student team, or panel of students to present some prepared material to the whole class. Although ESL teachers are accustomed to the use of group work in their classes, the tasks typically assigned in ESL courses are just as often along the lines of language analysis and language practice activities. In contrast, the types of student-to-student discussions more frequent in mainstream college classrooms tend to directly focus on challenging subject matter tied to content area topics. In an EAP oral communication course, speaking and listening tasks are tied not only to understanding but also to learning content area information, concepts, and principles. These are the kinds of abilities you need to be prioritizing.

Remember that Students Must Be Able to Speak Up during Whole-Class Lectures

Although other formats for learning are used in mainstream classrooms, most of the time professors teach by lecturing to the whole class. This is a pervasive format for college teaching. The norms of whole-class lecturing have changed, however, over recent decades. Increasingly, college lecturers have been developing ever more participatory styles for interacting with groups of students. That is, lecturers expect class members to take part in give-and-take discussions that are more interactive, more dialogic, and less like the traditional monologues you and I may have experienced as college-age learners.

Teach Students to Interact with Lecturers

Because college teachers expect students to participate along with everyone else in the room as a lecture-discussion unfolds, EAP learners are challenged to contribute frequently during lectures. They must be able to ask questions, request clarifications, voice confusions, provide original examples, and in other ways contribute to the quality of the professor-led discussion. Be direct in teaching students how to be participatory in these ways. The challenge is to teach EAP learners how to interact with college lecturers. One could argue that the most important role you will play in the course is to assist learners in developing their abilities to speak on substantive topics with college instructors and L1 classmates. These abilities lie at the very heart of learning to speak for academic purposes.

Discuss with Learners the Changing Norms of College Classrooms

Many of your students may be the first members of their families, or of the first generation, to attend college. They may have poorly informed or unrealistic ideas about the norms of discussion in college classrooms. Talk with them about the styles and formats of teaching that are prevalent within university classrooms. Bring in video clips of college lecturers in action, or just take the time to talk about such things. Help students recognize that an essential part of the learning experience in class is to express oneself through speaking, including speaking up, and using speaking-to-learn behaviors during the midst of a college lecture.

Learn to Recognize Differences between Different Kinds of EAP Learners

Many things work against the academic success of second language speakers. The level of language proficiency may be problematic, the interpersonal situation may be unfamiliar, and a learner may be tired, overworked, or distracted because of some personal matter. The student may even resist the content focus of the course, the instructional materials, or the teaching style. Some students may be reluctant to work with other class members or may object to the very idea that they will have to learn to speak up more often in class. Some students just want to be left alone so that they can work out their preferred learning strategies on their own.

Many factors can work against a learner's comfort level in an EAP classroom setting. Some, though certainly not all, students in EAP or other ESL college preparatory programs may have relatively advanced English conversational skills. These students are generally competent in interpersonal skills and can speak with relative ease in familiar social situations. Such students may be long-term residents of the United States and/or graduates of U.S. high schools. However, they may feel less at home with the kind of speaking that should be the target of the EAP oral communication course. At the other extreme, some students may be more recent arrivals to the United States and may be less confident in most situations of spoken communication. It is helpful to keep differences between such groups in mind.

Learner Characteristics: Length of Residence

An important learner characteristic to know is length of residence and schooling in the United States prior to entrance into your course. Generally, it takes six to seven years of schooling in English for an ESL learner to do well in college courses beyond ESL courses. This is a considerable period of time. When I say "six to seven years of schooling in English," I mean mainstream content area course work—through some combination of high school and middle school—in challenging academic subjects such as science, social studies, math, and literature/language arts. Students who have lived and gone to school in the United States for fewer than six to seven years or who have not attended English-medium schools for at least that long are less likely to have developed the requisite study skills in English for successful college-level work.

Academic study skills take much longer to develop than general conversation skills in a new language. Therefore, part of your role is to challenge students to improve their academic study skills and abilities. This information helps explain why some learners may seem quite competent when participating in social conversations in English but may be poorly prepared for academic success.

Some other students are more recent arrivals to the United States. A few may possess impressive study skills as a result of strong secondary and middle school educations in their native countries. It is worth finding out if their prior education in content area subjects was conducted in their native language or at English-medium schools. In the case of the former, students may possess studying-to-learn abilities in the native language that they are now being challenged to apply in English. Students who have attended English-medium schools in parts of the world where English is not a dominant language may continue to face significant challenges as English speakers. These students may seem weak in speaking and listening in English but may be relatively strong in reading and writing because of prior training in these areas. Recent arrivals who have only studied English in English-as-a-foreign-language courses may take even longer to apply study abilities developed in the native language to the experience of learning directly in English. On a practical level, you may find yourself teaching a course that includes a mixture of the following:

A. Longer-term residents of the United States who attended high school or middle school for six or more years in this part of the English-dominant world

B. Shorter-term residents of the United States who may have attended some high school or middle school in this part of the world but who have fewer than six years of such prior schooling in English

C. More recent arrivals who attended high schools and/or middle schools at institutions in their home countries where English was the primary medium instruction

D. More recent arrivals who may have studied English as a foreign language in their home countries but who attended high schools and middle schools where the primary medium of instruction was the native language

To gain a clearer understanding of your students' strengths and weaknesses, it is worth gathering this kind of background information. One way is to feature relevant items on general information sheets you have students fill in on the first days of class. For example, *In what year did you begin to live in the United States? Where did you attend secondary school? What was the language of your secondary school education?*

As speakers and listeners for academic purposes, the longer-term residents of group (A) may develop as strong EAP learners if their study experiences in English provided appropriate challenges and lasted for at least five years. Some drawbacks are that the quality of schooling in English may have been less than adequate for college success. They may have been strongly influenced by social and other nonacademic distractions all too familiar at American high schools. Students from group (A) may also seem more confrontational in the classroom, more demanding, and less open to an instructor's teaching if it conflicts with their prior expectations. These students may be very fluent in the spoken English used for conversational and social purposes.

For the shorter-term residents of group (B), if they have resided in the United States for fewer than five years, they probably have had insufficient time to develop the study skills to succeed as college-level learners in English without EAP support. As their instructor, it is important for you to realize that they may be capable of eventual success but that they ran out of time in their preparation at the secondary school level. They may need another year or more of EAP training. Your job is to assist them in further developing and refining their study-to-learn abilities in English. They may need even more time to develop these abilities than students of group (A).

Long-term residents who attended some combination of high school and middle school in the United States for seven years or longer typically score out of EAP courses on language assessment measures. They usually enter mainstream college courses directly with little need for EAP support. However, you may find some students with this profile in your course. They are even more likely to be unhappy as members of your course and may be very vocal in expressing their displeasure. Be aware that complications in learning to function well as college-level learners other than those normally associated with language-related matters may be at play. Be patient with such learners, but also seek outside advice (e.g., from academic counselors and other colleagues) on how best to handle their particular needs.

Students in group (C) are also in strong positions to develop along a normal developmental trajectory as EAP learners because they have sustained experiences in learning to study in English. Their conversational use of English may be less fully developed than that of students from groups (A) and (B). It is worth remembering, though, that they have significant background as English-medium learners. The schools they attended were probably private and their families' socioeconomic backgrounds relatively high. Thus, the quality of their prior educational opportunities may be stronger in some ways than those available to students from group (A) or (B). Students from group (C) may be unaccustomed to working with learners who more openly question or challenge the authority and/or expertise of course instructors. Although they may not appear as capable as English language speakers relative to the members of group (A), their progress in developing EAP speaking and listening abilities might surprise you by the end of the course.

Students in group (D) may reflect some of the strengths of those from group (C). For the most part, though, these students are learning to use study skills in English for the first time. If the secondary and middle schools they attended were strong, they may already have developed requisite study skills in the native language. A significant challenge before them is to apply and further develop such abilities in English. Although they may have studied English as a school subject for many years, their experiences in content area courses will have been in a language other than English. It is worth remembering that they are developing conversational uses of English while they are also learning to apply in English what they already know about learning academic subject material. Such students are likely to be more accepting of your style as a teacher, although they may be more comfortable with a more authoritative teacher presence in the classroom.

Chapter **5**

Why Are We Studying How to Speak English?

FEATURED IN THIS CHAPTER

- What to do when students wonder why they are in the course
- Differences between speaking for social and academic purposes
- A role for video recordings of lectures
- How to build learner awareness of EAP speaking needs

As discussed in Chapter 4, some students you meet will have been living and studying in the United States (or some other part of the English-speaking world) for an extended period. Many may have completed most of their high school studies within English-medium settings. Such students may have strong opinions on why they do not need to take "yet another course" that they perceive to be centered on "how to speak English." What they probably do not realize, and may take some convincing to believe, is that their English language skills may be quite strong in speaking for general social purposes but may be less reliable in communicating for academic purposes. At the start of the course, lead students to recognize how the kinds of speaking-to-learn and listening-to-learn behaviors they must develop to succeed in college involve sets of abilities that merit special attention.

Speaking in English while socializing is not the same as speaking for academic purposes. Simply being able to talk or engage in small talk during class time is not the point of your course. It does not even come close. The abilities you need to foster, encourage, and teach directly are academic speaking abilities that go well beyond small talk and casual conversation. At a very simple level, when making contributions during class, students must learn to ask relevant questions while demonstrating awareness of appropriate levels of course content. They also must be able to voice confusion and request information. At such times, they need to be appropriately polite and respectful toward everyone in the room, especially their peers. Although it is fine for a student's question to reveal only partial understanding of the content under discussion, the question does need to be informed by what has been going on in the course. In addition to asking appropriate questions, students also need to paraphrase what others have said, contribute thoughtfully to discussions, be respectful of others' opinions, and so forth. Early in the course, introduce the concept of *speaking-to-learn.* Draw contrasts between speaking-to-learn and other purposes for using spoken language. Remind students of important differences between casual conversation with friends and the special types of speaking that take place in academic settings.

Comparisons between Speaking for Social and Academic Purposes

Engage students in comparing the uses of spoken language for social and academic purposes. The two styles of speaking may have important elements in common, but they are not the same. Find out if students have any experience in speaking about academic topics. What kinds of speaking tasks were common in their previous schooling? What were some things they did as speakers in secondary school? Did they ever have to give in-class reports? Have they ever appeared in a role-play or play or participated in a debate in either English or their other language? Get them to talk about any experiences they had while in study groups alongside monolingual speakers of English. Have they ever studied challenging course content in their native language(s)? Can they distinguish between the following types of speaking, which take place in various settings: in the cafeteria, at a dinner table, in a car with friends, in a study group preparing for an exam, during small-group discussion tasks, during a visit to an instructor's office, while interacting with an instructor during a lecture on an academic topic?

SOCIAL AND ACADEMIC PURPOSES FOR SPEAKING ENGLISH

An In-Class Task

Ask students to generate a list of all possible situations (settings and related tasks) in which they speak English. Students usually respond well to such activities. They typically have a much easier time generating a list of social purposes settings, and that is an important purpose of the activity. But also remind them that speaking for academic purposes occurs in particular settings that are not as familiar as most of the less formal locations in which they speak and listen to English. Have them divide their list under two major headings. Along a left-hand column, have them list settings that are more casual and informal in nature. Along a right-hand column, have them list the settings that are more academic in nature.

For example:

Walking in a park with a friend	Asking a question in a classroom
Over lunch	Participating in a debate
At a dinner table	Speaking up in public
	Taking advantage of office hours

Guide the class in distinguishing between speaking for general social purposes and speaking for academic purposes. Start with the following table, and ask them to add to the lists.

Social Purposes	Academic Purposes
Small talk	Focus on particular content
Embedded in "here and now" topics	More context independent
More personal	More formal
Colloquial uses of language	Tied to abstract topics
Speaking to maintain social contacts	Speaking to learn concepts and to explore ideas
Fewer listeners to what we say	Larger number of listeners may be present when we speak

Draw parallels to reading-to-learn and writing-to-learn abilities: Discuss with students the concept of reading-to-learn because it may be more familiar to them. Ask them to make two lists of reading materials: academic reading material (reports, essays, nonfiction textbooks, journal articles, book chapters, specialized magazines) and nonacademic reading material (greeting cards, signs, recipes, comics, popular magazines, *TV Guide,* novels read for pleasure). Most students have little trouble coming up with items for at least the second category. Explain that while reading-to-learn at the college level, they will have to do more than simply comprehend the materials. Reading for comprehension is an important basis for college work. Beyond that, however, they will also need to remember, learn, synthesize, and analyze challenging content from assigned reading materials. Design similar discussions around characteristics of "writing-to-learn" as well (note taking, drafting as part of essay writing, writing short-answer responses to exam topics).

Once the concepts of reading-to-learn and writing-to-learn are clearly established, involve students in defining and providing illustrations of what you mean by speaking-to-learn. The kind of speaking that takes place in academic settings includes the kinds of casual teacher-learner conversations already familiar to ESL students, but it also extends well beyond such speaking styles. College students are expected to participate in content-focused discussions, question-and-response interactions with teachers and peers, panel reports, participatory lectures, and other types of speaking-to-learn activities. Remind the class that just as they must develop reading-to-learn, writing-to-learn, and listening-to-learn abilities as college learners, they must also become comfortable with the speaking-to-learn tasks and responsibilities that play major roles in mainstream courses.

Collaborate with the class in proposing a succinct working definition of what you mean by speaking-to-learn. Through small-group work or whole-class discussion, ask class members to generate their own definitions of the concept. Be sure to require that they include illustrations. One way to set up this activity is as follows:

> You have entered a first-year college-level course titled World History. The course is organized around assigned readings from a core textbook, and class meetings feature plenty of instructor-led discussions and lectures. Everyone is expected to read assigned chapters before coming to class. The instructor both lectures to

the class from the front of the room and leads the whole class in discussion and analysis of assigned reading material. Your task is to define and give illustrations of the kinds of speaking-to-learn abilities you will have to master to succeed in such a course.

Divide the class into groups of four to complete this task. Give them ten to fifteen minutes to work together. Later, you can (a) ask a representative from each group to summarize their discussion and illustrations or (b) engage the whole class in further discussion of the topic.

Minimally, illustrations of speaking-to-learn that should emerge from the discussion are students' abilities to:[1]

- *Ask questions for clarification*
  - "I think I understand this part, but could you . . ."
  - "I'm sorry, but I was not able to hear what you just said. Would you be able to repeat that?"
  - "The other day you mentioned that our next paper should be about twelve pages in length, but in the syllabus it suggests a sixteen-page limit. Could you talk more about the papers and just how long they should be?"
- *Summarize a point the instructor has made*
  - "Okay, let me see if I understand this clearly. What I think you are saying is . . ."
- *Interrupt politely*
  - "Excuse me for interrupting, but . . ."
  - "Pardon my interruption, but I wonder if you . . ."
- *Make requests*
  - "I'm sorry, but I cannot see the overhead very clearly. Can you adjust the focus a bit?"
  - "I remember that you said something about ____ last week. Could you go over that again? I missed it in my notes."
- *Express confusion*
  - "I am having trouble understanding that part. Is there a way for me to understand it better?"
  - "I'm not sure I understand what you just said."
- *Agree with a point someone has made*
  - "I agree with what you just said. I also think that . . ."
  - "That's a really good point he just made. Could we also relate that to yesterday's discussion of economic theory?"

- *Ask for a paraphrase*
  - "I think I understand, but could you explain that in another way?"
  - "I'm sorry, could you paraphrase that?"
- *Disagree politely and respectfully*
  - "Oh, okay, I think I understand the first point, but when you said ___, isn't there another way to look at that? For example, I was thinking that . . ."

I will return to such categories in the next chapter.

Once you and the students have established that speaking-to-learn abilities are real, identifiable, and genuinely needed for academic success, the purpose for your general work in the course can begin. Focus on teaching students how to develop these abilities. The pedagogic literature on second language strategy instruction implies that speaking-to-learn strategies must be taught explicitly. Your role is to (a) define and model speaking-to-learn strategies for students, (b) give each strategy an explicit label (a name), and (c) provide many opportunities during class for students to practice each strategy. An essential means to provide such opportunities is through academic mini-lectures designed for these purposes. During the course, you will need to provide many opportunities for students to better understand, develop, and practice their abilities in speaking-to-learn. Class configurations to explore should include the following:

- Whole-class lectures that you deliver live and through which you present challenging content material to the class
- Invited lectures provided by visiting mainstream course instructors
- Video-recorded lectures presented for similar purposes (use these sparingly because they are not live)
- Whole-class discussions
- Small-group discussions
- Simulations of visits to instructors' offices during office hours
- Opportunities for students to work together in study group sessions
- Panel discussions in which a subset of students participates at the front of the room
- Student presentations in teams at the front of the room (two or three students working together)

- A student presenting alone at the front of the room (single-speaker-format)
- Tasks in which students learn to leave concise voice mail messages
- Poster sessions
- Video projects produced by teams of students
- Reports on surveys students have conducted outside class
- Library reports
- Reports on public lectures attended on campus

All these formats should be explored as means for enhancing learners' speaking-to-learn abilities. Engage students in tasks through which they identify and discuss similarities and differences between relevant speaking-to-learn behaviors across the various configurations presented. Leave room in your course syllabus for as many speaking-to-learn forums as possible while being responsive to the priorities you have set. Review the bulleted list of class configurations and tasks listed above. Rank order them according to what you perceive learners' needs will be in mainstream courses at your college.

As a next stage in your illustration of speaking-to-learn abilities, ask a content area instructor to present a lecture to your class. Invite the guest instructor to give something along the lines of an introductory lecture. Tell your students they will be quizzed on some of the content covered. Ask the instructor not to hold anything back but to speak to the class as if those present represented a typical population of college students. Content area lectures from such disciplines as history, sociology, art, music, psychology, and biology are particularly appropriate for such purposes. If anything, explain to the visiting instructor to speak at a level slightly beyond the students' current levels of listening and speaking proficiency (although most lecturers tend to do this even without prompting).

Before the lecture begins, challenge students to demonstrate that they can keep up with the lecturer by asking relevant questions, by responding to the lecturer's prompts, and by paraphrasing essentiai points from time to time. Also, remind them that they should take written notes on the content introduced. As the visitor lectures, observe the class and take notes on what your students can and cannot do. Use what you learn while observing for subsequent lesson planning and discussion.

Following the lecture and the lecturer's visit, invite students to comment on what the experience was like. Were their language abilities challenged? Are they able to review and comment on some of the content covered? Are their notes comprehensive, and could their notes be used for subsequent study purposes? Explain that in an upcoming class they will be quizzed on some of the content. Provide opportunities for individual and/or small-group review and discussion of the lecture's content. In study groups, have students formulate possible questions you could include in a test bank of items.

Use Video Recordings to Illustrate Some Characteristics of Academic Lectures

At some colleges, in-house video recordings of authentic lectures given in content area courses are available. More commonly, they are difficult to come by. If such materials are available, arrange to work with them in your course. Another possibility is to produce such recordings in collaboration with colleagues. Internal funding programs through faculty development programs such as Instructional Innovation and Improvement of Instruction Grants are sometimes available for such purposes. Learn about the availability of such programs, and collaborate with others to better position yourself to apply for such support. Otherwise, several commercial sources provide academic lectures on videotape.

For example, the commercial enterprise The Teaching Company makes video and audio recordings available of whole college-level courses from a wide range of academic disciplines (http://www.teach12.com/). In this series, a complete course titled Thomas Jefferson: American Visionary consists of twelve lectures, each thirty minutes long. The set of twelve lectures is relatively inexpensive ($60 in 2005). Sets of lectures for at least thirty other content areas are also available. These are rich resources for illustrating some characteristic features of academic communication. Select a lecture series, and use excerpts in your class to illustrate differences between social and academic styles of spoken communication. Ahead of time, review fair use limitations of such materials, and be sure to comply with any copyright restrictions. The point in working with video recordings of academic lectures is to expose EAP learners to such discourse styles. Then they can begin to see that the quality of spoken language in college classrooms presents challenges that are different from those more familiar in social situations.

In Chapters 8 and 9, I discuss drawbacks to working with videotaped lectures in EAP courses, but the context of my comments is different in those chapters. Briefly, I believe that EAP learners must be presented with live academic lectures in EAP courses frequently and that there is no substitute for the interactive dynamic between members of a class and their instructor. Academic lectures made available from enterprises such as The Teaching Company, however, can be useful for building learner awareness of academic discourse styles. They provide opportunities for learners to observe and analyze how lecturers speak and can be beneficial when used judiciously to introduce EAP learners to distinctive features of lecture discourse. My reservation in working with such resources is that the use of recordings in EAP classrooms does not provide opportunities for the kinds of verbal give and take between lecturer and students that are essential parts of more interactive styles of college teaching. As an alternative or complement to using video recordings, arrange for students to audit several mainstream course meetings, as well.

Set the Right Tasks

Ask students to take descriptive notes on what they notice as they attend a live lecture or watch one on videotape. For example, how long are the lecturer's speaking turns? Who else speaks? Do students ever contribute? Do any features of language seem special in any way?

Challenge students to characterize some of the differences between the speech styles a lecturer might use when addressing a whole class and the speech their friends might use in casual settings. Ask them to think about both the listening and speaking abilities they would need in order to learn academic content efficiently in such a setting. Most students are readily aware of the need to develop listening abilities, but their awareness of their needs as EAP speakers tends to be less fully developed. Discuss strategies they must master as speakers to participate interactively with their teachers and classmates during lecture phases, discussion phases, and follow-up study group sessions that are integral parts of academic course experiences.

Another good way to build learner awareness of EAP speaking needs is to give a lecture yourself and to pause intermittently for students to ask questions, paraphrase key points, raise related topics, and so forth.

Be direct in telling them what you are doing, and ask them to contribute during the pauses. Remind students that if your pauses are met with not much more than silence from the group, then, as a class, there is much work to be done. This is, of course, one reason they are enrolled in your course. Also remind them that if only a few members of the class live up to expectations for participatory interaction during a lecture, then the others in the room are not rising to the challenge of mainstream courses. Approach these topics with appropriate tact and common sense. Your purpose is not to worry or discourage students but to present realistic challenges they can live up to. Engage students in discussions of what they can do to further develop such abilities. For example, invite students to visit the following Internet site made available by the University of Minnesota: http://www1.umn.edu/ohr/teachlearn/int/resources.html. It provides hundreds of audio-recorded illustrations of the kinds of questions undergraduate students typically ask of their instructors. Encourage students while also reminding them that your purpose is to be direct in teaching them what they must be able to do as English language speakers to succeed as college learners.

Endnote

1. The illustrations of speaking-to-learn strategies featured in Chapters 5 and 6 were initially inspired by a presentation in Steer, J. 1995. *Strategies for academic communication.* Boston: Heinle & Heinle.

Part **3**

Native English Speakers (Instructors and Peers)

Chapter **6**

Getting to Know Course Instructors

Teaching appropriate ways to interact with college instructors both inside and beyond the classroom really must be a priority in your course. Students who succeed in college are those who find ways to develop constructive working relationships with their instructors. In general, most college students, including ESL learners, tend to undervalue how important it is for them to get to know their instructors and the essential role such contacts play in forming and maintaining learning partnerships. Even students who realize the importance of developing and maintaining contacts with their professors may not have the personal resources to follow through on their best of intentions. It is imperative, however, that students learn to feel more comfortable around college faculty; they will have to interact with instructors frequently on both substantive and casual matters and in both formal and informal settings.

Often, ESL students think it is only part of their instructor's responsibilities to get to know their students and to express interest in how well their students are getting along. But the reality is that college faculty are busy people who differ in how conscientious they are when it comes to getting to know the many students who cross their paths. Because faculty-student contacts are essential to learning, students benefit if they play a proactive role in this regard.

An important role you can play as an EAP instructor is to guide learners in how to initiate and maintain positive working relationships with content area faculty. At the very least, students need to feel comfortable communicating with instructors both inside and outside the classroom. By all means, set aside time to discuss these issues with your class. Design classroom tasks that provide learners with tools for initiating and maintaining both public and private conversations with their professors. The time you spend in this area will be well worth the effort. Remember, one of the clearest indicators of student retention in college is the success the individual student has in forming and maintaining at least one continuing working relationship with at least one faculty member. Such connections really do make a difference.

Things You Can Do

Discuss the importance of student-faculty relationships openly with your class. This is one topic teachers rarely discuss with EAP learners. Lacking such discussion, learners may never realize how important constructive contacts with faculty can become. An effective strategy is to be direct with students and to speak with them about how important their interactions with course instructors can be. Remind them that you are not referring to yourself in particular but that you want to prepare them to get to know mainstream faculty they will meet this term and in the future. Explain that research on college-level retention indicates students who form at least one sustained connection with even a single mainstream instructor over time are more likely to take their studies seriously, to stay in college, and not to drop out of school. Your course can go far in ensuring that EAP students can initiate and maintain constructive working relationships with at least some of the faculty whom they will meet during their college years.

Aim to increase students' awareness of just how busy instructors' lives can be. College students have many misconceptions about the roles and responsibilities of faculty. It is well worth the effort to discuss faculty responsibilities in the areas of teaching, research/publication, and professional service. Talk about your own experiences as an instructor and some experiences of your colleagues. Find relevant articles from publications such as *The Chronicle of Higher Education* to introduce and discuss with the class.

I am always surprised by the enormous gap between the reality of faculty responsibilities and students' perceptions of just what those responsibilities might entail. I have met many students who believe that college instructors have relatively soft, cushy jobs once they are established in their careers and that faculty really do not have to work all that hard. Other students may have equally extreme misconceptions of an opposite nature. They might avoid getting to know their instructors because they think faculty members are too busy for such things. These attitudes tend to change once students get to know the faculty better. By depicting at least some aspects of what faculty lives are like, students will have a clearer appreciation for their instructors' professional responsibilities. At the same time, remind them that one of a faculty member's first responsibilities is to the students enrolled in his or her courses.

As a starting point, involve students in identifying strategies for getting to know their instructors in ways that are respectful of everyone involved. Have students read and discuss the following list of strategies for getting to know their instructors. Later, ask learners to brainstorm and append items to the list. Engage them in conversation about ways that college students can get to know their instructors better. Some learner strategies you might suggest that EAP students begin to use include the following.

Things Students Can Do

- Introduce themselves and make a direct personal contact at the end of the first day of class.
- Remain in class until most of their classmates have left the room, and see if it is an appropriate time to engage the instructor in casual conversation.
- If the instructor is walking back to the office, offer to accompany her or him along the way.
- Always maintain an appropriate professional distance during their conversations with instructors.
- Take advantage of the instructor's office hours by visiting early in the course.
- Help ensure that both the student and the instructor feel safe and secure when they are conversing in private. For example, if a student is visiting in an instructor's office, the student needs to be sure that she or he has left the office door wide open as they enter the room.
- Avoid any romantic involvement with an instructor. Life is complicated enough.
- E-mail the instructor after the first day of class with a brief message that includes a physical self-description and brief biographical self-introduction (the student's purpose is to make it easier for the instructor to learn her or his name).
- Make it a point to sit near the front of the room.
- Maintain an appropriate degree of eye contact during class.
- Volunteer to assist the instructor in mundane tasks such as raising blinds, opening windows, or erasing the chalkboard, as appropriate.
- Be well prepared for class.
- Raise their hand and offer to respond to general questions directed to the whole class.
- Politely ask questions and request clarifications when something seems unclear.

Invite a Content Area Instructor to Visit Your Class

An effective series of classroom tasks might culminate with a subject-matter instructor visiting your class. The purpose for this kind of visit is not to give an academic lecture but for students to get to know the instructor better as a person as well as a professional. In days leading up to the visit, prepare students by planning questions they can ask and topics to discuss with the instructor-visitor. Ask the visitor to talk about and provide an overview for one course she or he teaches. A useful focus is a course your students are likely to take in the future. While discussing the course, the instructor might talk about general expectations, reading load, suggested study strategies, possible solutions to time management issues, productive use of office hours, related course policies, and so forth.

Students would benefit from discussing with the instructor appropriate and inappropriate in-class behaviors, names or titles to use when addressing instructors (these change, depending on the time and setting as well as local expectations and norms), and pet peeves regarding student behaviors or past performances, among other concerns. Students can practice speaking-to-learn behaviors by asking the visitor questions. Whenever you devote class time to these topics, focus discussion on just how many opportunities college students have to initiate conversations with faculty. Provide opportunities for students to propose their own ways of getting to know their instructors better.

Teach Students How to Interact with Instructors for Academic Purposes

As you may have already surmised by now, the theme developed in this part of the book lies at the heart of what an EAP oral communication course is all about. To succeed in college, ESL learners must be able to interact with their professors and classmates. By being able to speak for themselves in class, they will become better known by their professors, better able to affect the pacing of lecture delivery, more likely to find satisfactory answers to their questions, and enriched by their experiences as college learners.

Teach Speaking-to-Learn Behaviors

Talk to students directly about their getting to know their instructors. Consider the following as the basis for a script when speaking to the class. Modify and expand it to suit the learning preferences of your class:

> Let's talk about speaking-to-learn behaviors. One thing I'd really like you to get out of this course is the realization that you must be able to speak up for yourself in class in order to succeed as a college student. There is no getting around this, especially in academic courses beyond our EAP program. You might perceive yourself to be shy or poorly prepared to speak up in class, but you really need to grow beyond such self-perceptions. To be honest, they are not very helpful. At appropriate times, you need to speak up in class while using effective speaking-to-learn behaviors. I am using the phrase "speaking-to-learn" deliberately. In everyday life, you might not think of speaking as a tool for learning, but in college classrooms that's part of what is taking place all the time. Speaking-to-learn behaviors will serve as integral parts of your classroom learning experiences. During an academic lecture, for example, you might speak up in class to ask a question. When you do, you are having an impact on what your professor is saying, how he says it, as well as his pacing and delivery. In fact, just by asking the question you have influenced the pacing of the lecture and perhaps its sequencing of topics. Beyond that, you have also given the lecturer an opportunity to gauge realistically just how well her or his messages are getting across. So you see, even a simple question can serve important purposes in a mainstream college classroom.
>
> As your college career continues, each of your instructors needs to recognize you as a member of the class. They need to know that you are engaged in and serious about learning the material covered in the course. They need to know that you are capable of participating and that you are thoughtful enough to do so from time to time. College professors depend on your contributions, and your speaking-to-learn behaviors present essential opportunities for your professors to get to know you better. An indispensable way for you to be part of the

classroom learning process is to contribute in appropriate ways during whole-class lectures, small-group discussions, office hour visits, and other opportunities to speak.

Part of the challenge in learning to speak up during class is to treat the instructor and other classmates with appropriate levels of politeness and respect. The goal is to learn to interact with everyone in the course in a respectful and thoughtful manner, both inside and beyond the classroom. Being respectful should be a central feature of your speaking-to-learn behaviors. People need to hear from you, and they also need to perceive that you are a pleasant person whom everyone will enjoy getting to know better.

Another thing to keep in mind is that most of the time, most college instructors realize all too well when they are having trouble communicating their ideas successfully to the class. You know the feeling. When a professor's messages are not getting across, there is a general sense of everyone being somewhat uncomfortable in the room. Usually, the communication problems a lecturer might be having in getting messages across are obvious to everyone in the room. You can make a constructive difference when such complications occur. Class members who use supportive speaking-to-learn behaviors during class discussions and lectures and who do so to make the instructor/professor and everyone else "look good"—or at least better—and to make everyone in the room feel more comfortable are more likely to be successful in the course. Everyone benefits when you contribute in thoughtful ways to whatever might be the messages the instructor is trying to get across.

Building upon illustrations first introduced in Chapter 5, here are additional purposes and examples of supportive speaking-to-learn behaviors. They are intended to assist all those in the classroom in making the most of an instructor's efforts to lead an effective lecture and discussion. All students must learn polite ways to speak with professors or classmates when it seems necessary to:

- **Interrupt** (e.g., *"Excuse me for interrupting, but . . .";* *"Pardon my interruption, but I wonder if you . . .";* *"I am sorry to step in like this. I hope you don't mind, but there is something you just said that I'm not sure I understand. Can you . . .?)*

- **Ask a question for clarification** *("I think I understand this, but could you . . ."; "So far, I think I understand, but I was wondering if you could clarify that section on . . .")*
- **Summarize a point someone has made** *("Let me see if I have this. What you are saying is . . ."; "Okay, I think I have it. Do you mean that . . .")*
- **Agree with a point and then introduce a related point** *("I agree with what you just said. I also think that . . ."; "Yes, I agree when you say that . . .. It also reminded me that . . .")*
- **Ask for a paraphrase** *("I think I understand, but could you say that another way?"; "Is there another way to say that? I really am trying, but I am not sure I understand.")*
- **Disagree politely** (It is okay to disagree with someone else's opinion, including an instructor's, as long as you find a way to do so cordially. *("I think you're right when you say . . ., but isn't it also true that . . ."; "The part about . . . seems reasonable. No one could argue with that, but when you got to the part about the . . ., I'm not sure I agree with you there."; "I know I might have this wrong. Could you clarify?")*)

In general, students listening to a lecture should be trying to keep up with what is going on interactively in the classroom by asking themselves self-monitoring questions such as:

Is this a convenient time for me to speak up in class by:

- *summarizing some of the content being explained?*
- *asking a question?*
- *requesting a clarification?*
- *providing a new and different example?*
- *asking for help?*
- *pointing out a relationship between ideas that I recognize but that other members of the class may be missing?*

Prepare Them for Mainstream Settings

As an EAP instructor, try to better prepare students in your course by:

- Engaging them in collaborative classroom tasks in which they expand the list of speaking-to-learn illustrations in each of the sections previously listed.
- Giving them plenty of time to propose original wording for the various question types presented.
- Asking them to expand the list of headings so that students end up proposing additional language functions not listed here.

For students who have opportunities to sit in on content area courses, ask them to write down in a notebook some examples of the kinds of questions they hear other college students use in the classroom. Ask them to focus on questions students ask of their professors when the class really seems to be engaged in the material. Explain that they need not focus on all the language included in a student's question (that would be too difficult a task in any case). The focus should be on the openers, just the first few words the questioner uses. How does the student get the professor's attention? What phrases does the student use to initiate her or his turn to speak? What words or phrases are used to signal a polite manner of speaking? Once you have gathered examples from your students, see if they can classify the questions they have gathered according to the scheme presented in this section. If they cannot, engage the class in proposing additional categories for the kinds of questions college students really do ask in class.

To provide direct instruction in the kinds of speaking-to-learn behaviors I am advocating here, lecture and mini-lecture to the class on substantive topics on a regular basis. When you do, use opportunities to teach interactive strategies directly. Prior to the lecturing phase of the lesson, explain to the class that you expect them to interrupt you from time to time. Challenge students to develop their own interior sense of when and how to interrupt politely.

In preparation, set up classroom activities in which learners practice the kinds of sentences and phrases they might use. Give them opportunities to expand their lists of options. When you first start the lecture, use pauses as clear indications of moments when you would like someone to ask you a question. Also pause and provide opportunities for students to practice other speaking-to-learn behaviors you are interested in teaching. Be up front and explain directly that you are doing this. Teach students to make effective use of the pauses you provide. Explain that later in the course, you will provide fewer pauses while you lecture and that students are to become more capable of interrupting you on their own. Distribute a list of phrases students could use to initiate questions during your lecture. Make sure they have the list in front of them, and ask them to use it to initiate questions while you lecture. Show your appreciation when someone uses an effective speaking-to-learn behavior.

Once a mini-lecture is over, review some of the more successful instances in which a student had something to say. Celebrate students' successes in learning to interact effectively with you and with their classmates during EAP lectures or discussions.

Chapter **7**

Interacting with Native English-Speaking (NES) Classmates

FEATURED IN THIS CHAPTER

- Why ESL students need to get to know their NES peers
- Complications in learning to do so
- Ways of fostering ESL-student to NES-student interactions
- A role for student opinion surveys
- The importance of inviting NES students to visit your course
- A role for former EAP students

The next step in their lives as college students is for your students to enter mainstream courses. Thus, it is essential that EAP learners develop self-confidence in studying with classmates who are native English speakers (NES)—that is, peers who are *not* ESL learners. Many second language learners of English fall into the habit of letting NES peers do most of the interactive work in the college classroom setting. At the same time, college learners, whether NES or ESL, want the time they spend in discussion and study groups to be productive. Time is a valued commodity in North American culture. A potential danger is that NES sometimes tire of working with ESL classmates who are less capable as participating members of study groups. At such times, ESL learners may find themselves missing out on potentially valuable opportunities to work alongside NES peers. When this happens, ESL learners are disadvantaged in several ways.

First, they lose important opportunities to engage with and learn the content material of the course. Second, they miss out on opportunities to develop mutually supportive classroom relationships with NES peers. Third, they miss out on essential linguistic opportunities to progress as language learners if their verbal interactions with NES are limited. Finally, ESL learners may miss chances to make fuller social connections beyond the classroom with NES, a highly valued dimension of college experiences in North America.

Some Things You Can Do

This is yet another area in which you can make a difference by discussing the issue with your class. You can also develop an original mini-lecture on the topic. At the very least, assist students in recognizing the problem. With most groups of ESL learners, though, either students are already aware of the need to learn to work effectively with NES peers or it takes very little convincing for them to recognize this need. A more difficult stage is for you as their teacher to do something about it. A starting point is to set course tasks that require the formation of study groups outside class time. Even if only with ESL classmates, students need to learn how to make necessary contacts, organize, and work efficiently within study groups for academic learning purposes.

Arrange for Native English Speakers to Visit the Class

Another helpful thing you can do is to invite NES learners to visit your class to discuss their experiences as college students. Connect with matriculated college students who are close in age and life situation to the members of your class. While arranging for a visit, prompt the visitors to discuss their own perspectives on what it has been like to work with ESL learners as classmates and study partners, including whatever might be their frustrations and apprehensions. Encourage these NES visitors to explain frankly what they perceive to be advantages and disadvantages of collaborating with ESL learners for academic study. Ask them to talk about complications they may have faced when working with ESL learners as classmates in content area courses.

In advance of such visits, prepare your class to ask relevant questions. This preparatory work is an essential stage. Give ample time and attention to preparation activities in class. This could be tied to a set of assigned tasks for students to work on in study groups outside class. What ESL learners will want to know are ways they can get to know NES classmates better and how to become more integral participants as members of mainstream courses and study groups. Schedule several such visits with different NES college learners across the time frame of your course. Ahead of time, engage the class in a sustained discussion of what they would like to know and how they will phrase their questions. On the day of the visit, emphasize the need to be polite and friendly while they are speaking with visiting student peers even if some of what they hear is disheartening or unclear. Remind them that the visitors will not be language teachers but NES college students similar in age and experience to themselves.

Have Your Students Survey Opinions of Matriculated NES Students

Another useful activity is to require your students to interview (and in other ways to interact with) matriculated English-speaking college students. This is a good way to create projects and related activities that expose EAP students to peers who are NES speakers. It is important that learners recognize a focused purpose for such tasks. Some activities might first ask learners to design a survey on the topic in class as a group or whole-class project. The idea is to prepare them well during class time before sending them out to meet NES on campus. After they have settled on the information they want to gather and have practiced asking survey questions, send them out to conduct their field work on campus with NES as survey informants. Such a survey might address a content area topic featured in your course, or it could be even more direct by featuring topics related to NES college students' perceptions of working with ESL classmates in mainstream courses.

When designing and planning to conduct a survey on campus, your students may collaborate with members of a different course that enrolls large numbers of NES. One possibility is to work with an academic support course offered through other departments. Other mainstream courses that can serve for these purposes include both introductory and advanced courses in general communication, cross-cultural communication, anthropology, and sociology. Collaborative projects designed in conjunction with faculty from such disciplines would permit ESL and NES learners to participate in joint projects while working side-by-side generating survey items, gathering information, and reporting back the results of their survey activities.

Although it is essential that students work their way through the process of designing an appropriately worded survey and survey items for themselves, here is an initial topic to clarify for possible informants. It is followed by examples of items that might be included on a class survey.

AN IMPORTANT TOPIC TO CLARIFY AHEAD OF TIME

I am going to ask you a series of questions about people like me who are non-native speakers of English. In the survey, I will refer to us as speakers of English as a second language, or even simply as ESL speakers. *ESL* means people like me who speak English as a second language.

Before we get started, do you know anyone beyond our campus who is a non-native speaker of English? Do you know any students here on campus who speak English as a second language?

[Note to whoever is conducting the survey conversation: Leave ample time to clarify who ESL speakers are before going on with the survey. Once you are sure this is clear, continue.]

Examples of possible survey items:

- Are you taking any courses in which there may be one or more ESL classmates?
- Have you ever had conversations with any of them?
- Do you know any of their names?
- In your estimation, how well do they speak English?
- Can you name one course you have this term in which there are relatively more ESL classmates than in any other course?
- How about previous terms?
- What is your impression of the ESL classmates you have noticed? Are they good students?
- Have you ever worked with any of them?
- Can you describe any opportunities you have had to speak or work with any ESL classmates?
- What are some advantages of having ESL classmates in the course?
- Can you discuss any disadvantages of having ESL classmates in the course?
- Have you ever worked with an ESL classmate in a small group, one-on-one, or as part of a course project?
- If so, can you talk about what the experiences were like?
- Was your ESL classmate able to "pull her or his own weight" during your collaboration?
- What advice might you give to an ESL classmate who wanted to participate more actively in class?
- Can you discuss any ways in which an ESL classmate could get to know other members of the class better?
- Would you entertain the possibility of forming a study group outside class that included any ESL classmate? Why or why not? Have you ever done this?
- What do you perceive are some of your ESL classmates' frustrations as members of a college course?

An alternative set of survey activities might canvass parallel impressions and responses from matriculated ESL students who have moved beyond EAP support courses and are already enrolled in mainstream courses.

The possible survey items I have listed here are merely suggestive of possibilities. When planning such a series of survey activities, it is important that students discuss and generate their own bank of survey items. They need to be invested in the generation of the survey itself and of the items it features. A central concern is for you to prepare them well: Give them plenty of time to come up with appropriate topics for the survey. Provide plenty of practice opportunities in class so that EAP students can learn how to ask questions well and in other ways interact effectively with NES college students. It is counterproductive to send students outside the classroom before they are ready to do so.

Conduct Small-Group Discussions with NES College Students

Seek opportunities to include NES college students in small-group discussions with your class. Develop connections on campus that will permit you to coordinate your course with a course in your institution's Department of Modern Languages. For example, if your class includes many native speakers of Spanish, some NES learners of Spanish might be invited to participate with them in small-group discussions on a focused topic. If other language backgrounds are represented in your EAP course, NES learners of these other languages could be involved in a similar activity structure.

Invite Former ESL Students to Visit the Class

It is often useful to invite former ESL students who have been successful in mainstream courses to visit your class to discuss their experiences as college students. Prompt them to comment on strategies for working with NES classmates that have served them well. Get them to discuss both their disappointments and accomplishments in working with NES. Prepare your class well to make the most of such visits. Ahead of time, collaborate with students to generate a list of questions they can ask:

- What were your experiences like when working alongside NES in mainstream courses? Can you describe these experiences?
- Were the NES you got to know friendly? Describe how you know this.

- Did any problems arise?
- What strategies do you use to meet and get to know NES classmates?
- Have you ever had opportunities to work in study groups with NES?
- Were the study groups useful? What did you like best about them?
- Knowing what you know now, how could you make your time in study groups more effective?
- What is it like to have to study in English alongside NES?

An option is to share such a list of topics with the ESL visitors in advance of their class visit. Seeing the items ahead of time will give them time to think over and plan some ideas to discuss.

Part 4

The Role of Academic Lecturing

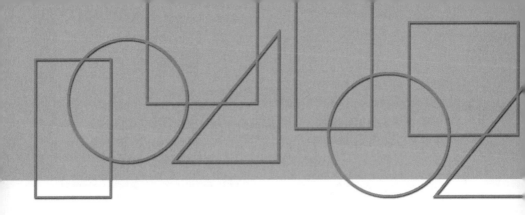

Chapter **8**

Prepare to Present "Mini-Lectures"

A major theme I emphasize throughout this book is the pervasive role of academic lectures as a form of instruction at the college level. Think back on the central roles that lecture and discussion formats played in your own undergraduate education. Contemporary models of college teaching have expanded beyond traditional formats of "chalk-and-talk" lecturing from the front of the room. For example, in many university classrooms, lecturing now includes other visual supports such as PowerPoint presentations, overhead projections, and slides. More interactive modes of college teaching are also gaining popularity. Yet, the general procedure of an instructor speaking to a large group of learners from the front of the room persists as a primary teaching mode.

Part of your role in the teaching of oral communication for academic purposes is to prepare learners for the challenges of using both listening-to-learn and speaking-to-learn behaviors during academic lectures. To prepare them well in these areas, you need to present mini-lectures to your classes on a regular and frequent basis.

The Role of Substantive Content in Your Course

To lecture in class for any sustained length of time, you need material of interest to talk about. If you have adopted a course text from the Houghton Mifflin oral communication series, you have access to sufficient content for the course. You can incorporate substantive content into an ESL or EAP course in many ways. Alternatives include content-based, theme-based, and task-based language teaching. Review what you already know about these ways of infusing content into language courses and apply them in your teaching. Although not always possible, an effective option is to decide on a single content focus for the entire course. Or, if such an approach is not workable in your program, try to feature a series of related topics, each of which can be used for a series of five to eight consecutive classes.

In an ESL oral communication course I recently taught, for example, the content focus for the course was human communication. All the mini-lectures I included in the course were tied to this topic. I found the focus on human communication to be especially useful because so many resources were available. Textbooks used in departments of communication as core reading materials in introductory courses, for example, provide plenty of varied materials for this course content focus. I collect and use such textbooks to identify lecture topics and to assign reading materials in preparation for mini-lectures. Other ESL oral communication courses might focus on such areas as psychology, sociology, and intercultural communication. Texts of the Houghton Mifflin oral communication series feature themes of human psychology in Book 1, connections between human beings and animals in Book 2, communication and media in Book 3, and money in Book 4.

Whatever the overarching themes of the course might be, identify the content of mini-lecture topics early to give yourself enough time to prepare. When planning the course, try to schedule a series of academic mini-lectures on a regular basis. In most courses, two twenty-minute lectures per week will probably suffice.

The act of lecturing in classrooms is held suspect by many people, including ESL teachers and learners. Early in the course, discuss with your students the importance the role of lecturing will play during their undergraduate years. One way to begin such a discussion is to ask students to describe some of the instructional formats they think they will encounter in academic courses they will be taking. Students already enrolled in mainstream courses can comment on the formats of courses they currently are taking. Ask the learners if they have ever listened to an academic lecture. Prompt them to describe the experience and to discuss what it was like for them as learners.

Near the start of the course, provide a lecture on the process of taking notes during an academic lecture. A useful focus for such an early lecture is to give advice on effective listening-to-learn strategies. Search the Internet, your institution's library, or any good bookstore for resource materials. Many such resources are available, and they provide rich bases for developing a lecture on this topic.

Ellis (2000),[1] in the Houghton Mifflin series, includes an in-depth discussion of the following (and many additional) topics designed to develop undergraduates' academic listening and related note-taking abilities. Try using some of Ellis's topics as a basis for creating one of your first mini-lectures in the course. If you prepare to spend one to three minutes discussing and illustrating the importance of each point listed below, you will have a complete fifteen-to twenty-minute lecture on the topic. You might introduce the lecture as "suggestions for developing listening-to-learn behaviors." Ellis proposes that any college student who wants to develop effective listening-to-learn abilities needs to learn the importance of the following:

1. Completing assigned readings ahead of time
2. Bringing the right materials to class (text, notebook, pen and pencil)
3. Sitting front and center in the classroom
4. Conducting a short preclass review of the material to be covered
5. Clarifying one's intentions as listeners in college classroom settings

6. Accepting and learning to live with the mind's tendency to wander
7. Noticing what one's written notes look like and making changes as necessary
8. Staying in tune with ("being with") the instructor
9. Noticing one's environment
10. Postponing debate and suppressing the impulse to question everything the lecturer says
11. Letting go of judgments about lecture styles
12. Participating in class activities
13. Relating the class to one's future goals
14. Thinking critically about what one hears
15. Being alert to repetition
16. Listening for introductory, concluding, and transition words and phrases
17. Watching the board, overhead projector, or any information displayed
18. Watching the instructor's eyes
19. Looking out for and taking advantage of obvious clues to topic development
20. Noticing the instructor's interest level

Use such a listing of listening-to-learn suggestions and corresponding resource material to plan a single lecture or a series of four- to five-minute lectures sequenced for the first few days of the course. If handled wisely, such presentations can serve as effective starts to the course.

Lecture Live to the Class

As useful as audio and video recordings can be, when it comes to lecturing to a class there is no substitute for live delivery in the teaching of EAP oral communication. Live lectures have the advantage of providing learners with opportunities to use and practice listening-to-learn and speaking-to-learn behaviors. In an earlier chapter, I mentioned that videotaped lectures could be useful as consciousness-raising tools. They can illustrate some of the discourse conventions that academic lecturers use. But the live medium offers an added essential dimension of the messages you should be presenting in the course. Thus, it is counterproductive to depend too much on either audio or video versions of lecture material. I feel strongly about this. In fact, I prefer live lecture delivery even if audio- or video-recorded versions of lectures are available as part of an assigned textbook's instructional package.

Classroom teachers can do considerably better than merely using available technology to present recorded lectures to students. A better way is to prepare ahead of time to lecture live with the support of either a written transcript or written notes. I say this because ESL learners preparing for academic study must learn to cope with the live delivery of academic lecturers. They need as many opportunities as possible to learn to interact with a lecturer while practicing speaking-to-learn behaviors.

In my experience, audio and video recordings fail to provide opportunities for the kinds of authentic participation that students need to practice in preparation for the real thing. It may be easy on the teacher to pop a video or DVD recording into the classroom's media station. But recordings of lectures leave a lot to be desired for those interested in teaching speaking-to-learn behaviors. By their very nature, recordings provide prerecorded information only. Some essential dimensions of listening-to-learn and speaking-to-learn behaviors can only be made available when there are opportunities for students to ask questions and in other ways to interact with lecturers directly, live and in person. Recorded lectures do not provide students with the best opportunities to acquire listening-to-learn and speaking-to-learn abilities.

Working with a Publisher's Lectures and Lecture Transcripts

Of course, many sets of EAP instructional materials designed for courses at this level feature recorded lectures as audiotape, videotape, CD, or DVD recordings. In many classroom textbooks, written lecture transcripts are also featured as additional support materials. Many teachers find them helpful. Personally, I enjoy working with them but not in the ways probably envisioned by the developers and publishers. When used in creative ways, these materials can serve as useful resource materials. But I suggest that, even when such resources are on hand, you avoid the temptation to depend on audio or video recordings as substitutes for live lecturing. At best, the use of a recorded lecture would be a second-tier choice.

A Common Dilemma with Recorded or Transcribed Lecture Materials

Many sets of ESL and EAP instructional materials feature recorded academic lectures, as well as written transcripts, at the back of the book or in an instructor's manual. If you have access to such resources, you have some tough decisions to make. Sometimes whole chapters in a textbook are tied to a coherent, carefully structured, and consistent presentation of the lecture material as featured in the instructional package. Let's assume that, as you examine the instructional supports, the recorded lectures seem useful, their recorded quality is appropriate, the transcripts are reliable, and you have easy access to them. As you examine the textbook, you realize that the process of students working effectively with the tasks and activities featured in the book is dependent on their first having been presented with the lecture material. Sometimes the learning tasks and activities assume that students have been presented with a lecture exactly as featured in the instructional resources. Even though I am calling attention to the importance of lecturing live to the class, the course textbook is structured around the presentation of a fixed lecture. Under these circumstances what should you do?

You have several choices. First, you could ignore one of my major themes in this book and simply play the recordings to the class. This option is especially tempting because the inclusion of visual and audio presentation of a lecture seems, at least on the surface, to simulate a real classroom experience. But depending on playing any recording in class is a choice I caution against for reasons previously discussed. Most important, students are missing opportunities to practice speaking-to-learn behaviors and related strategies for interacting with a lecturer. I am convinced that live lectures need to be a central feature of any EAP oral communication course designed to teach either speaking-to-learn or listening-to-learning abilities.

A second but better choice would be to remind yourself that you are capable of delivering the lecture live to the class. Learning to deliver a lecture to a group of EAP learners is a challenge, but it is not as difficult a challenge as it might first seem. You have the necessary skills and supports. You have access to the recorded lectures and/or lecture transcripts. Thus, a way to address the dilemma is to become as familiar as you can with the content of the prepared lecture material. If audio versions are included in the instructional package, use them to your advantage. Work with them in private, but treat them as part of your own preparation resources, not as a main event inside the classroom. I suggest that, starting a few weeks before a planned lecture, you listen to the recordings while traveling to or from work (some teachers do so while exercising) with the aid of a portable audio player. Knowing the content of such material well is a great asset in preparation for lecturing live to the class.

In a later chapter, I focus on options for developing your own academic lectures and lecturing supports. In the next section, I discuss ways to proceed when an instructional package already includes a fully developed set of lecture materials.

Some Words of Caution

All teachers have preferences for the supports they like to have on hand when speaking in front of a group of learners. Although it may not be your favorite way of doing things, one option for lecturing live is to work closely with transcripts provided by a publisher. I mention this option at the risk of violating some of the most common and valuable pieces of advice usually given to instructors of mainstream college courses. The support literature on college teaching advises lecturers to suppress the impulse to lecture verbatim from a prepared script. Most course instructors feel disengaged from the materials if they are simply reading from a written text or script. This disengagement tends to happen when working with a script because teachers are not as invested in what they say. Everything has been prepared ahead of time, the language is fully elaborated, they are trying to be careful with their enunciation, their eyes are tied to the page, and the danger is that they may lack spontaneity in their delivery. As a consequence, mainstream college instructors who address their classes in this way sometimes fail to convey that they are thinking deeply about the topics they are presenting. Students notice a teacher's lack of investment and may begin to feel disengaged from the material as well. Also, the act of simply reading prepared material aloud interferes with maintaining needed eye contact with the group. The teachers are casting their voices down toward the script instead of looking up as they speak.

A Better Option

Mainstream college lecturers are usually advised to work from an outline, talking points, or notes on index cards. In preparation, lecturers can structure outlines around major ideas, important phrases, and keywords. When speaking from an outline or list of talking points, teachers tend to sound more extemporaneous. They are expressing themselves more directly to their listeners. They are more in tune with the gathering of personalities before them. An outline is especially useful in organizing a talk and in providing an overview of its general structure. By including a list of talking points, a lecturer is better prepared to speak more extemporaneously, especially if she or he knows the material very well. Additional visual supports such as a flow chart of main ideas, semantic map, concept map, or tree diagram can be useful for depicting a sequence of ideas to include in the lecture. Whenever possible, take the time to create such lecture supports.

At times, you may prefer to speak more extemporaneously in front of the group by working with an outline, index cards, a series of talking points, or a visual map you can refer to when needed. My focus in the next few paragraphs is somewhat different. The options I discuss in this next section can be combined with one or more of the options just introduced. I am returning to the context in which (a) you have access to recorded lectures and/or written transcripts and (b) as the teacher you realize that these materials need to be presented in the course. If your instructional materials feature such supports, there are ways to work with them productively while remaining true to a preference for live lecture delivery.

Preparing to Actually Deliver a Scripted Lecture

Sometimes it is necessary to work with lecture materials included in the course textbook and instructional supports available from a publishing company. When I decide to work with transcripts, for example, my first step is to make a clear photocopy of the original transcripts. When photocopying, I take the time to enlarge the copy. Even if your eyesight is particularly keen, enlarging the copy makes it much easier to use the material as a necessary support when lecturing live. I do so to be able to maintain more effective eye contact with the learners once I begin to lecture.

After I have made an enlarged master copy of the transcript, I cut the text apart and arrange the written material into separate sections. My purpose is to reformat the text so that no more than one paragraph appears on a single page. Then, working with each of the individual paragraphs a second time, I photocopy each of these sections onto a separate sheet of paper. A lecture that lasts about ten minutes as an audio recording might be fifteen to twenty-five paragraphs in written format. Once I have completed photocopying the individual paragraphs, I use the resulting written script in class to facilitate a more interactive style of live lecture delivery.

Because each paragraph appears on a separate page, the script I carry in hand will be about fifteen to twenty-five pages of enlarged print. It is not that my eyesight is bad. I prefer to work with enlarged print because the transcript is very easy to read and to scribble notes on. More important, I find the size to be a clear advantage when speaking in front of a group of learners. Another tip is to sequentially number the pages somewhere easy to see, such as the upper right hand corner. This way, if you happen to drop, misarrange, or shuffle the pages, you can gather them together quickly and return all the pages to the correct order.

Use Structured Reviewing to Grow Familiar with the Material

Once the pages are ready, I work with the lecture for several days to become familiar with its content, premises, trajectory, transition sections, keywords, and other features. I want to know the material well to avoid sounding disengaged from it once I begin to lecture. In preparation, I adopt a study strategy known as *structured reviewing*. The idea of structured reviewing is to be deliberate in developing a schedule for learning to work with the material. It is similar to scheduling practice time when learning to play a musical instrument. On the first sitting, I read the material through twice. Then I wait a half hour or so before reading it through once more. While working this closely with a transcribed lecture, you can underline or highlight words you want to emphasize, scribble notes in the margins, place slash marks where you want to pause in your delivery, and in other ways prepare the materials in personal ways for live lecture delivery. I write on the pages and insert my own thoughts and examples to make the material more my own.

Structured reviewing comes into play by planning your time deliberately for working with the lecture's content. For example, I might spend thirty minutes with the transcript on the first morning, twenty minutes with it later that afternoon, twenty minutes on the second morning, ten minutes later that afternoon, ten minutes on the third morning, five minutes on that afternoon, five minutes on the fourth morning, and so forth. Even when you add up all your preparation, it is not all that much time to have spent getting ready for an in-class lecture. The process usually takes less than two hours overall.

The idea is to revisit the material at regular intervals but for manageable periods of time while reducing in stages the amount of time you devote to the materials. It is the same principle piano teachers apply when they explain to their students that it is more effective to practice in three twenty-minute periods spread across an entire day than to practice sixty minutes in a single sitting. Preparing to work with a lecture transcript through structured reviewing follows a similar principle.

By the time you are ready to deliver the lecture, you will know the material well. You will have worked with it many times in private. The pages will be marked with annotations and special notes on lecture delivery. Additional examples of key points may have been added. In general, knowing the material well permits you to be more at ease and to use a more participatory lecture style. Once you are in front of the class and have the copies of the lecture in hand, you are ready to begin. Your performance as a live lecturer will be more useful to learners than any videotaped material might have been.

Be Up-Front and Explain to the Class What You Are Doing

Before you begin the lecture, explain to the class that you will be working from a written script but that your intention is to engage them in as participatory a manner as possible. Remind them that you are a language teacher first and not a specialist in the content area that happens to be featured in the course. Be sure the class understands that you use the content area to provide opportunities for everyone in the class to develop requisite listening-to-learn and speaking-to-learn abilities.

Explain that you want them to interact with you during the lecture by asking questions, requesting clarifications, paraphrasing from time to time, providing their own examples of ideas presented, and so forth. That is, remind them that you want them to be participatory by using speaking-to-learn behaviors they have been learning and practicing in the course. Once everyone understands these ground rules, you are ready to begin the lecture.

Maintain as much eye contact with the class as you can. You have the script before you, and it is perfectly reasonable to refer to it frequently. Because I know well the scripts I work with and the print is large, I like to carry them in one hand and move freely around the room from time to time while lecturing.

Any sections from the script you speak aloud should be delivered as naturally as possible. Although the process of working with a lecture transcript may sound awkward as described here, eventually you will develop your own lecturing style. If you are conscientious in your preparation and in the use of structured reviewing techniques, you will be able to deliver a prepared lecture featured in published materials more extemporaneously. In the next chapter, I focus on preparing lectures of your own design based on original preparation.

Endnotes

1. Ellis, D. 2000. *Becoming a master student* (9th ed.). New York: Houghton Mifflin.

Chapter **9**

Develop Your Own Lectures and Lecture Supports

As emphasized throughout the book, one of your major challenges is to develop students' abilities to be full participants as speakers in mainstream courses. To do so, students need to possess strong speaking-to-learn abilities. That is, they need to be able to speak up in class in order to interact with their teachers and peers. To prepare them in these areas, you must provide learners with opportunities to listen, learn, ask appropriate questions, voice confusions, and express themselves for other interactive purposes within a supportive environment that simulates the demands of content area courses. In Chapter 8, I discussed options for lecturing when recorded lectures and lecture transcripts were already included in your set of instructional materials. Another indispensable way to prepare EAP students in listening-to-learn and speaking-to-learn behaviors is through lectures you have developed on your own and present live in the classroom.

One complication is that most ESL teachers are not especially experienced as academic lecturers. In fact, lecturing is not a skill featured in most ESL teacher training programs. Even the very act of lecturing is held suspect in many educational circles. Several reasons can be proffered. Contemporary models of second language teaching emphasize communicative interactions between and among learners as much as between learners and their teacher. For very good reasons, this contemporary paradigm of language teaching sometimes leads to reduced amounts of "teacher talk." Efforts to reduce teacher talk currently reflect a widely recognized theme, and in most ESL settings efforts of this kind are appropriate and well worth the effort. But there is an alternative issue when you are charged with teaching the speaking-to-learn and listening-to-learn abilities that need to be featured in EAP programs.

In EAP oral communication courses, you are working with a specialized group of learners with particular needs. Many will already possess relatively strong oral language abilities, especially when they are communicating with peers for social purposes. They need to work on the particular forms of speaking-to-learn and listening-to-learn abilities that EAP learners require for success as college students. Not only do they need to learn to speak for themselves in academic settings, but they also need to cope with the demands that academic lecturing places before them. In short, they need to learn to be interactive with their professors when lectures are being presented. They also have to learn to discuss, with their peers in study groups and with instructors during office visits, the substantive content material presented to them.

Mainstream courses at the postsecondary level across the United States and Canada feature instructor-centered lecturing and demanding reading assignments tied to lecture presentation. These are essential forms of content presentation with which learners must cope for college success. In preparing students for such instructional formats, there is no substitute for live lecture presentation. A difficulty, however, is that taking on the role of an academic lecturer is a new professional challenge for many ESL teachers.

Know the Material and Become Comfortable with It

Whatever the content focus of your course, start early to become as familiar with the material as you can. Remember that you are a language teacher by training, interest, and experience. Although you may have some interest in them, the content areas featured in the Houghton Mifflin oral communication series (human psychology, connections between humans and animals, communication and the media, and money) are probably not your primary areas of expertise. But you need not be a specialist in these areas or in whatever content area might be featured in your course. Your area of expertise is language teaching. The content area of the course you are teaching serves as a necessary medium for using your knowledge as a language teacher to improve students' listening-to-learn and speaking-to-learn abilities. You already have one or more college degrees, are well read, and know how to work with ESL students. By reading ahead, gathering additional resource materials, and doing your homework in preparation, you will develop a sufficient knowledge base to lecture well to the class. The time and energy you put into preparation will pay off when you make your presentation in front of this particular group of learners. And you will be even better prepared the next time you teach the same course.

Discuss Your Strengths and Weaknesses as a Lecturer with Students

Your students will get to know you well through the time they spend with you in the course, at least in this one dimension of who you are as a language teacher. There is no denying this fundamental fact of the role relationships between students and teacher. Especially the first time you teach the course, there is no reason to present yourself as anything other than who you really are.

You are unlikely to be a specialist in the content area(s) the course happens to feature. Let students know that first and foremost you are a language teacher. Be clear about your reasons for including academic lecturing as an integral part of the learning experiences in your classroom. Explain to students that participating in the kinds of lectures you will be incorporating into the course will prepare them for academic success in the future. Your focus is to teach listening-to-learn and speaking-to-learn abilities. When the content of a lecture moves beyond your level of knowledge, be straightforward and discuss this issue with students. They will respect you more if you are direct and honest with them about what you do and do not know. You are not, after all, a specialist in the content area you will be highlighting in the course.

If students ask questions to which you do not have ready answers, let them know you will research the topic and come back to the next class better prepared to respond. At times, look for opportunities to turn some of the responsibilities for conducting such outside research over to students. Solicit student participation with prompts such as, "Who would like to learn more about that topic and report back to us in a later class?" Students may respond even better if you offer extra credit—or some other extra perk—to anyone who researches a topic successfully, especially if the topic is of special interest to the class.

Plan to Lecture for Short Periods of Time

Even for native speakers of a language, attention spans as listeners are limited, especially when listening-to-learn in academic settings. In your course, your most effective lectures will be relatively short. If a lecture lasts for more than about twenty minutes, class members are likely to become distracted, anxious, and even bored. You will have reached a point of diminishing returns after about twenty minutes, perhaps even sooner. Learn to use students' facial signals, body language, and your own intuitions as a language teacher to gauge the class's attention span. Timing and sequencing are especially important here. Although you might begin a class with a review or previewing activity, an efficient use of class time is to feature a lesson's lecture phase as close to the start of class as you can. You might explore the option of lecturing at the class midpoint, but you will probably find it ineffective to wait until the last twenty minutes of class to begin a lecture. As far as deciding to sequence the lecture into the day's overall lesson, a good rule of thumb is to get students while their minds are still fresh and open to your presentation style.

Set Realistic Expectations about What Can and Cannot Be Accomplished during a Lecture

The purpose for featuring mini-lectures as a part of the course is to provide opportunities for students to develop listening-to-learn and speaking-to-learn abilities. It would be counterproductive to inject massive amounts of new information into a twenty-minute lecture. Rather, aim for a handful of major points you can discuss and review during the lecture several times. Although I like to experiment with and use alternative formats for lecture supports, the strategy of limiting a lecture to a handful of eight to ten talking points usually suffices as a support for an in-class EAP lecture.

Structure Your Talk in Three Phases

Follow some of the advice often given to lecturers in mainstream courses. Most content area lecturers are familiar with this well-known format:

1. Tell students what you are going to talk about (give them a preview/synopsis up front).
2. Go ahead and tell them (deliver the body of your lecture).
3. Tell them once again what you have just covered (provide a summary and review at the end).

This three-part structure is commonly featured in content area classrooms where lecturing is frequent.

Lecture Preparation

If you are working with one of the books in the Houghton Mifflin oral communication series, the content areas for the course are set by the instructional materials. The same will be true for most EAP course texts, even the materials from other publishers. Over the span of the course, you will probably want to include a mix of lectures based on publisher-provided resources and at least some supplementary lectures of your own design. For teachers creating an entire course on their own, the process of developing their own lectures is even more central to their planning. My focus in this section is to discuss options for developing original lectures.

In any EAP course, you need to become as comfortable as possible with the content areas and themes featured in the course. Draw upon whatever resources are at your disposal. Look for Internet sites devoted to the content area featured in your course. Certainly, read through the textbook that students will be purchasing for the course. Beyond that, visit the college's library and gather any related materials that may be available. Often, an introductory college level text or a few popular magazines may serve to supplement the content included in EAP materials. For example, listed below are some illustrations of where to turn if you are working with one of the course texts of the Houghton Mifflin oral communication series.

EAP Topic Area	Outside Resources to Supplement a Course Text
Human Psychology	■ Intro college-level textbooks in psychology ■ Back issues of popular magazines such as *Psychology Today*
Human Beings and Animals	■ Intro college-level textbooks in sociology and anthropology ■ Back issues of popular magazines such as *Nature* and *Scientific American* ■ Broadcasts from PBS's *Nova* series and The Learning Channel
Communication and the Media	■ College-level textbooks in communication, especially the many textbooks available for an introductory course in communication
Money	■ Intro college-level textbooks in finance and economics ■ Back issues of popular magazines such as *Money Magazine, Forbes, Consumer Reports*, and *Fortune* ■ Newspaper articles on related topics

Consult with faculty members who may be specialists in the content area featured in your course. Ask them to suggest sources for preparing a few lectures of your own design. If you will be teaching your course long term, consider auditing one of the courses to beef up your knowledge base and to witness firsthand the interactive dynamic of a content area course. While learning more about course content, review the materials you have on hand and gather ideas from colleagues who may have taught the same course or area of content in the past.

A few weeks before the course starts, begin to settle on what content you want your course to cover. In many cases, the textbook will determine general areas of content, but you may want to supplement text materials or change the sequencing of chapters. Decide on a tentative listing of topics and their sequencing. Estimate how much time or how many days of class to devote to any particular topic. These can always change once the course begins and you gain a clearer sense of students' background, preferences, and preparedness. It is important, however, to start off with a general plan subject to later deviation.

Part of your effort should be to organize into a meaningful sequence the topics featured in the course and course materials. Students will respond better to the content you cover if they can perceive an overall organizational plan. Alternative organizational plans such as topical, causal, sequential, structural, and problem-solution plans can be used to arrange sequences of presentation.

Plans that follow a topical sequence are commonly used in most EAP courses. *Topical organization* divides the overall course into a series of major topics to be covered and treats each topic in turn. A challenge to you as a lecturer is to find connections between the various topics to be presented as the course unfolds. Students are likely to appreciate both your own attempts and opportunities to draw connections between topics featured later in the course with those introduced earlier. Also look for opportunities to preview upcoming topics related to the course's current content focus. In their discussion of the "6-Ts" approach to EAP content teaching, Stoller and Grabe (1997)[1] offer many ideas on how to draw connections between the various topics of a topically organized instructional plan. They refer to these connections as "threads," and their explication of how to develop threads that connect seemingly unrelated topics is fascinating.

Sometimes chronological order can be used to sequence the presentation of course material. For example, there may be an easy-to-recognize chronological order in the development of particular schools of psychology, systems of government, or economic theories. In such a course, you would have the choice to organize course content according to a timeline of the initial development and subsequent widespread acknowledgment of particular schools of thought. EAP courses that feature history topics often use chronological order to structure the presentation of course materials.

In a problem-solution organization plan, the course could present a series of problems to be discussed or solved one at a time. Courses that focus on contemporary social problems, for example, might apply a problem-solution sequence. Several weeks each might be devoted to identifying, discussing, and then exploring possible solutions for such social problems as hunger, homelessness, racism, war, poverty, health care, immigration, and mental disease. The search to find connections between such social problems can become a recurring effort in the course. Stoller and Grabe's model for organizing a content-infused language course is also relevant here. Whatever organizational pattern seems implicit in the content featured in the course or whatever pattern you decide to follow, share your vision for course organization with students. Explain it to them early on and remind them frequently so that they can recognize how the various content segments are organized.

Expository Lecturing

As you begin to prepare individual lectures, a major factor to consider is learners' attention spans. The attention span of native English speakers is not much more than fifteen to twenty minutes. Use this information to guide you in deciding how long you would lecture to a group of EAP learners on any given day. Fifteen to twenty minutes is a reasonable period of time to plan for lecture presentation.

A straightforward expository (chalk & talk) lecture is probably the presentation style that learners will encounter most frequently in mainstream settings. Therefore, prepare learners for this style. Expository lectures are useful when presenting information explicitly and introducing broad concepts. They are less useful for getting learners excited about course content. These kinds of lectures are relatively passive experiences for learners because most of the information is laid out before them with little need for them to think critically or analyze concepts for themselves. The format is important, however, because content courses use it extensively. It represents one of the real-world criterion tasks for which you are preparing students to cope. Some significant demands that expository lectures place on students are reflected in learners' attempts to make sense of and create written notes from the material presented. Learners must be able to use their notes for study purposes.

More Learner-Participatory Lecture Styles

As necessary complements to expository lectures, you will want to develop more interactive styles of covering content material with learners. Whole-class discussions, case teaching, and Socratic methods of problem posing present even more efficient opportunities to develop students' speaking-to-learn abilities. These more participatory alternatives share the teacher's attempts to involve learners as active contributors to discussion during class lectures. Rather than using a transmission model to explain information in a didactic manner, the teacher engages the class interactively through discussion, brief role plays, and brainstorming sessions. The teacher in other ways also provides opportunities for learners to voice concerns, generate ideas, and explore possible solutions through illustrations, questions, and the instructor's continuing prompts.

In *case method teaching*, the teacher initiates discussion by describing a realistic situation in detail to illustrate a general principle or pose a series of problems. A case is a story the teacher tells as objectively and in as much detail as time will allow. The idea is for students to experience some of the complexities and uncertainties confronted by the original participants in the case. In an EAP course, for example, you could initiate discussion of roles and responsibilities of college faculty by describing a situation in which a student approaches an instructor about having trouble in the course. You have the time frame of a few minutes to introduce the case to the class. You would have to include as much detail as possible: (a) the student's and the instructor's life situations, (b) the nature of the student's problem in the course, (c) why the student felt compelled to approach the instructor for help, (d) any constraints or conflicts the teacher or student might be feeling, and (e) any other background information. The student, for example, visits the instructor at an inconvenient time when he or she was up against a looming deadline to submit a revised manuscript for publication in time for tenure consideration. Perhaps the instructor only has a few minutes before having to leave to chair an important committee meeting. At the same time, the instructor may remember that the student has a history of tardiness in the course, coupled with a confrontational attitude toward some classmates.

Cases are intended to be open ended and to leave room for an animated exchange of ideas. Subsequent to its presentation, you lead the group in a discussion of questions and issues suggested by the original case. In this and other forms of participatory teaching, the instructor's strategy is to engage the class in a meaningful exchange and development of ideas. Teachers pose questions, dilemmas, and provocative problems as a means for capturing learners' attentions and engaging them in course content. In a discussion of the evolution of forms of money, for example, a teacher might say, "What would our world be like if bartering were the primary means for buying and selling the things we use all the time in our everyday lives?"

Getting Ready to Lecture

Whatever lecturing style you devise for a particular day of class, here are some things to keep in mind. Most teachers are at least a little bit nervous the closer it gets to giving a lecture. Address any feelings of nervousness or tension by using whatever relaxation techniques are most familiar to you.

When I took speech courses in secondary school and college, I was trained to use breathing techniques to ease my nerves before speaking. The techniques were nothing complicated. The idea was just to use a few deep breaths coupled with a rising and lowering of the shoulders to ease tension in the upper chest and diaphragm. Some teachers learn to identify and then relax muscles in other parts of the body that may be tensing up.

Notice your own stress levels, and your preferred relaxation techniques. Also realize that controllable degrees of either anxiety or nervousness can have constructive facilitating effects when preparing to lecture. In manageable doses, they help ensure that you take your role seriously and that you will perform as well as you can.

Whenever possible, come to class a few minutes early to talk informally with class members. Get to know them as people, and give them opportunities to get to know you as well. Say something at the start of a lecture to catch your audience's attention. You could open with a provocative statement, an anecdote, or something that might surprise students and leave them in eager anticipation of what might be coming next. Aim for the time frame of no more than fifteen to twenty minutes. Keep issues of timing, sequencing, and transitions in mind. How fast should you be speaking? Learn to be deliberate in using pauses. Pauses can be purposefully manipulated for the entire time you are talking. They give students a few extra moments to understand what you are explaining. In which order will you present ideas and concepts? What transition words might you use as signals to the structure of your lecture? As well as a good opening, plan for an effective close to the lecture.

Rather than staring at whatever written supports you may have generated for the lecture, keep your eyes on the group before you as much as you can. Glance at your written notes when you need to, but spend even more time focusing on students and observing their responses. Engage in some one-on-one interactions with at least some members of the class. Interrupt your delivery often, and prompt one or more members of the class to ask a question, offer a summary of themes presented thus far, or pose a prediction of upcoming topic development.

It is important that your demeanor demonstrate that you are interested in and enthusiastic about the content you are presenting, even if you have private reservations. Students want to feel good about what they are learning and about your commitment to and personal engagement with course content. Try to be conversational in your delivery. As long as you focus on the meaning of the ideas you are trying to convey and on responses from your audience, you will come across as a conversationalist in your style of delivery. From time to time, move around the room. Play with your use of body language as a natural way to sustain student attention. Use your eyes, arms, and upper torso to lean into the audience and solicit their attention occasionally.

At the same time, avoid distracting verbal ticks or physical gestures that might pull your audience's attention from what you have to say. For example, students often become distracted by a lecturer who overuses verbal fillers such as "okay," "uhmm," and "uhh." These fillers rarely serve any constructive purpose. To find out what my own verbal fillers are—and like most teachers I have many—I like to audiotape myself every now and then while giving a lecture. There is nothing quite like hearing yourself as others hear you. A videotape can provide even more powerful information that is difficult to ignore, dismiss, or forget.

A Brief Note on Humor

Humor is a powerful tool in any language classroom. One challenge is to be open to humorous moments while stressing that you will not accept any words or behaviors that make another person the victim of malicious, or in other ways inappropriate, humor. A healthy attitude to project is that it is fine for everyone to laugh together when something funny happens but that no one should be permitted to laugh at the expense of anyone else. On the other hand, self-deprecating humor from the teacher usually works well, at least in North American college classrooms, as long as it is not overdone. Students appreciate knowing that you are comfortable in being able to laugh at yourself. Sarcasm, though, should be avoided. It is one of those conversation styles that never comes across well in language classrooms.

Endnotes

1. Stoller, F., & Grabe, W. 1997. A six-T's approach to content-based instruction. In M. Snow & D. Brinton (Eds.), *The content-based classroom: Perspectives on integrating language and content* (pp. 78–94). White Plains, NY: Addison Wesley Longman.

    This is an excellent resource. The authors are very clear in how to identify course themes that can be connected from one week to the next through the identification of macro-level content threads. It is an essential discussion of sustained content language teaching.

Chapter **10**

Questioning in Whole-Class Settings

Asking questions is one of the central roles instructors play in both EAP and mainstream college classrooms. Knowing how and when to ask appropriate types of questions, ones that will facilitate learning, involves abilities that are central to the teaching process. Moreover, the ways in which questions are posed illustrate questioning behaviors to students. By modeling sound questioning behaviors, instructors also help learners develop their own abilities to ask appropriate questions of their professors in content area courses.

Some of the central speaking-to-learn behaviors that students must master by the end of an EAP oral communication sequence are how and when to ask appropriate questions of instructors. To be active members of college classrooms, EAP students must be able to respond to and formulate their own questions and to anticipate the kinds of questions their professors will typically ask. While aiming to prepare learners in these areas, you should ask questions that spark learner interest, instill motivation, arouse learner curiosity, reinforce lesson content, and promote participatory learning. As mentioned in Chapter 5, the University of Minnesota provides an excellent resource making it possible for learners to actually listen to and explore the kinds of questions undergraduate students typically ask in class (along with instructors' responses): <http://www1.umn.edu/ohr/teachlearn/int/resources.html>. I encourage you to design tasks that require students to explore this and similar sites for themselves.

Begin with the Infusion of Substantive Content

To create an environment conducive to effective questioning behaviors, first you must have substantive topics to discuss. Whether your course is designed according to principles of communicative, task-based, content-based, theme-based language teaching, or some other instructional approach, at least some portions of the course must provide opportunities for students to learn via whole-class lecture and discussion. For students to learn to ask questions in class, they must participate in a course that immerses them within appropriately challenging areas of content. The content presented should include topics and themes spread out over a sustained period of time that will spark their interests and provide opportunities for genuine study and learning. If you are working with one of the course texts of the Houghton Mifflin series, you already have substantial content to work with.

Make Productive Use of a Question Taxonomy

Once the content area for the course or lesson is set, take some time to review Bloom's (1956)[1] question-type taxonomy. As widely used in education circles, Bloom's taxonomy categorizes levels of abstraction in the kinds of questions that are representative of classroom discourse. The taxonomy is useful as a structure for thinking about and learning to be deliberate about the kinds of questions posed by EAP oral communication teachers. A general teaching strategy is to begin with relatively lower level knowledge and comprehension questions. These are the easiest for students to handle. Equally important is to be purposeful in shifting between different kinds of questions, at increasing levels of abstraction, as discussion develops. The challenge is to present learners with as full a range of question types as is appropriate in a single class. Focus on being as direct as you can while providing instruction in this area. A simple strategy is to explain to students what you are doing. Tell them you are providing direct instruction in three areas:

1. How to ask better questions in class
2. How to anticipate their instructor's question
3. How to respond to instructor's questions

Teach the class labels for different question types. Provide practice opportunities for students to formulate questions of particular types for themselves. Share with students a copy of Bloom's taxonomy. Include brief pauses from lecturing in your teaching, and use these intermittent breaks to ask students to label or categorize the kinds of questions you have been using as well as the kinds of questions you would expect them to use. Remind them that you are familiarizing them with a full range of question types. Give them plenty of opportunities to generate their own examples of such questions. Explain that questioning behaviors in class are part of two-way communication: both teachers and students ask lots of questions. Stronger students are better able to formulate questions that help keep a lecture or discussion moving forward.

Discuss and practice timing issues with learners as well. What are some of the best times to ask questions? What are some subtle behaviors and body language that might indicate an instructor is ready for students' questions? Does the instructor's tone of voice or pausing patterns ever carry such signals? These areas are rarely taught directly in either mainstream or EAP courses. Assist students in recognizing that your course is different from other language courses they have had; you are providing direct instruction in questioning behaviors. As students begin to recognize such differences in course focus, discuss your purposes for teaching questioning and other speaking-to-learn behaviors with them.

Later in their college careers, students will encounter professors who ask questions of particular kinds and at particular levels of complexity. Some professors may fall into patterns of asking the same kinds of questions over and over again. Other professors may be more varied in their questioning patterns. Remind students that they can learn to recognize their professors' recurring question behaviors and preferred question types. When they can identify for themselves the kinds of questions their professors typically pose, they will be in a stronger position to perform well as participatory members of the class. Similar effects are likely to carry over into the kinds of questions professors include on quizzes and exams. What follows is a modified version of the six question categories Bloom provides, along with indications of the cognitive abilities targeted and illustrations of action words, question words, and model questions you can use within each category.

Bloom's Taxonomy*

Six Question Types Arranged from Lower to Higher Levels	Abilities Targeted	Action and Question Words to Feature _____ Model Questions
Knowledge	<ul><li>observation and recall of information</li><li>knowledge of dates, events, places</li><li>knowledge of major ideas</li><li>mastery of subject matter</li></ul>	list, define, tell, describe, identify, show, label, collect, examine, tabulate, quote, name, who, when, where, etc. What did you notice in this reading? How did the chapter begin?
Comprehension	<ul><li>understand information</li><li>grasp meaning</li><li>translate knowledge into new context</li><li>interpret facts, compare, contrast</li><li>order, group, infer causes</li><li>predict consequences</li></ul>	summarize, describe, interpret, contrast, predict, associate, distinguish, estimate, differentiate, discuss, extend Could anyone summarize the author's point of view? What was this reading about?
Application	<ul><li>use information</li><li>use methods, concepts, theories in new situations</li><li>solve problems using required skills or knowledge</li></ul>	apply, demonstrate, calculate, complete, illustrate, show, solve, examine, modify, relate, change, classify, experiment, discover Can anyone relate this information to current news events? Do you see any applications to your own life experiences?

Analysis	<ul><li>see patterns</li><li>organization of parts</li><li>recognition of hidden meanings</li><li>identification of components</li></ul>	analyze, separate, order, explain, connect, classify, arrange, divide, compare, select, explain, infer Who can point out some connections between these ideas and any of the other discussions we have had earlier in the course?
Synthesis	<ul><li>use old ideas to create new ones</li><li>generalize from given facts</li><li>relate knowledge from several areas</li><li>predict, draw conclusions</li></ul>	combine, integrate, modify, rearrange, substitute, plan, create, design, invent, what if?, compose, formulate, prepare, generalize, rewrite Given what we have learned in this reading, do we need to modify any of our earlier conclusions about X, Y, or Z?
Evaluation	<ul><li>compare and discriminate between ideas</li><li>assess value of theories, presentations</li><li>make choices based on reasoned argument</li><li>verify value of evidence</li><li>recognize subjectivity</li></ul>	assess, decide, rank, grade, test, measure, recommend, convince, select, judge, explain, discriminate, support, conclude, compare, summarize If someone asked you to explain this author's ideas to a skeptical audience that would likely doubt her or his basic point of view, how would you begin?

*Adapted from Bloom, B. S. (Ed.). (1956).

Create Questions and Write Them Down in Advance

In preparation for class, you will probably find it useful to compose a list of possible questions to use during the lesson. As you prepare, try to anticipate learners' responses and possible confusions. Once in the classroom, keep the list readily accessible. A useful strategy is to arrange such prepared questions on a single sheet. You will be able to carry the sheet with you as you move around the room, or place the list in front of you when you are seated at a desk.

Decide How You Will Ask Particular Questions

Teachers have several question-asking options. You can ask questions of the whole class, or question individual students. While exploring both options, you are simulating the way questions are used in mainstream courses. These are invaluable experiences with which students must learn to cope. Prepared questions sometimes may be projected on an overhead screen, divided up among small groups, distributed throughout the class, and student representative(s) may subsequently report back to the whole class. Effective teaching calls for an exploration of a wide range of options for using question in class.

Will You Call On Students Individually?

When asking questions, at times it is effective to pose a question to the whole class and then to wait until someone volunteers to respond. An advantage of this option is that the volunteer is likely to be ready and personally invested in her or his response. A drawback is that the same class members may contribute over and over again. Of course, there are always advantages and disadvantages to just about any questioning pattern.

A second option is to pose a question, wait a few moments, and then call on a specific student to respond. An advantage here is that, by naming a student, you may be helping to draw a less participatory member of the class into the discussion. Or, you may have a classroom management reason for addressing a question to a specific person. A drawback is that the individual you invite to respond may not be ready to do so or may feel too inhibited to have anything of substance to say.

A third option is to pose the question, wait a few moments, and then name rapidly three or four students. By naming them, the implicit message is that you anticipate at least one of these students will respond. Although you may expect only one of them to rise to the occasion, by naming several students in sequence, you reduce the pressure on any single individual. In this option, you limit the range of students being invited to participate while leaving it up to one of those three or four students to speak up before the others. Alternatively, follow the same nomination pattern but name the students prior to posing the question. If you do this, those three or four students will certainly be listening attentively to the subsequent question(s) you ask. At different points during a lesson, experiment with as many different options for soliciting student participation as possible.

Pay attention to how you ask questions, and try to balance the kinds of questions you ask. Most often it makes sense to begin with relatively simple and straightforward questions (e.g., "What was this reading about?" "Who can summarize the gist of what I was just saying?"). Then you can move on to questions that call for higher degrees of inference and analysis (e.g., "Given the information we have been reading and talking about, what do you think our elected officials should do about it?").

In committee work or in consultation with a colleague, share sample questions you plan to use in class. Ask for feedback and further suggestions. Periodically in the course, distribute a listing of some questions you have been asking. Give students opportunities to classify and group them in terms of Bloom's taxonomy. Beyond that, give students opportunities to identify some of the more useful questions that enhanced their engagements with course materials. Students' feedback on the kinds of questions you have used can guide your questioning behaviors for the future.

Turn-Taking Patterns in the Classroom

Any language class exhibits differences in relative degrees of active participation among its members. One way such differences are manifest is in *turn-taking patterns*. Speaking turns are particularly interesting and profitable for teachers to keep in mind. Who does the talking? Who speaks first? How are turns distributed? How do students interrupt each other to take the floor? Is one student's speaking turn ever stepped on or stolen by another student? As the teacher, do you ever step on or steal a student's speaking turn? Pay attention to turn-taking patterns and how turns are distributed in the classroom. They are rather straightforward to observe and recognize. Part of your role is to manage the class so that speaking turns are distributed as evenly as possible between everyone in the classroom.

An even distribution of speaking turns between and among students may be an ideal that is seldom realized. In the incredibly complex world of classroom life, some students are more outspoken and more participatory than others. All too often, teachers are unaware of such differences among students. Or, if they are aware of some of the more obvious differences in turn-taking behaviors, most teachers take limited steps to address the issue.

A necessary first step in learning about turn-taking patterns in your course is to define what constitutes a "turn" during classroom interactions. Teachers need some rough-and-ready parameters in order to recognize (a) what constitutes "a turn," (b) when one turn ends, (c) when another turn begins, (d) how long a turn typically lasts, (e) who takes more turns than others, (f) which students generally do not get their fair share of turns, (g) which students regularly step on or steal others' turns, and so forth. You can make a real difference when it comes to ensuring that turns are equitably distributed. One strategy is to build learner awareness of the impact of turn-taking patterns.

First, it is useful to discuss the phenomenon of turn-taking patterns with the class: Explain that you want as many people as possible to have opportunities to speak up in class. Mention that your ideal is for everyone to have an equal number of turns to speak during each class and during the course as a whole. Ask them if they recognize the phenomenon of turn taking. Have they ever thought about such patterns before? Have they ever been in any classes where one or two people dominated as contributors during class discussions? If they have had this experience, how did it make them feel? Often, students will have their own stories to tell about the impact of students who tend to dominate class discussions. By engaging students and asking them to voice their opinions and concerns on this topic, you will be starting the course off in the right direction.

A section of Chapter 17 is devoted to identifying the "action zone" of your course. Briefly, which students respond and interact with you most frequently? Once you identify them, take deliberate steps to reach out to others. Some ways of identifying such behavior patterns are to invite a visitor-observer to the room to keep track of student patterns of participation. Another way is to audio- or videotape whole lessons.

Endnotes

1. Bloom, B. S. (Ed.). 1956. *Taxonomy of educational objectives: The classification of educational goals: Handbook I, cognitive domain.* New York: Longman.

Chapter **11**

Class Sizes and Configurations

FEATURED IN THIS CHAPTER

- Why students need to learn about the effects of different kinds of classrooms
- How class size and furniture affect learning opportunities
- Ways to build learner awareness
- The "open-U" configuration to facilitate communication

Not all college classrooms are created equal, and students need to learn about some of the differences between them. Teach students to recognize that class size and furniture configurations really do affect classroom dynamics. Some mainstream courses take place in small seminar rooms with fewer than twenty students. Other courses may be taught in very large lecture halls. Here are a few physical configurations representative of college classrooms.

In some courses, students sit around a table with an instructor who might be positioned at the head of the table. One of the most common configurations is rows of students in seats, with the instructor at a large desk in front of a chalkboard or near a screen at the front of the room.

Some classrooms are very large lecture halls resembling the kinds of amphitheaters featured in the movie *The Paper Chase*. Teachers may stand or remain seated at the front of the room, or they may be much more active in moving around the classroom. In rooms of moderate size, some instructors prefer to have all class members seated in a circle or semicircle, with the potential for everyone to face each other directly. Some classrooms have numerous computer stations mounted on fixed desks. Others feature a single computer screen at the front of the room that everyone can see at the same time.

It is important that EAP students be aware of the many ways classrooms can be organized and the impacts these formats have on the potential for interactive learning and teaching. Discuss with students some advantages and disadvantages of different configurations. Be sure they realize that the nature of participation patterns an instructor might expect in the course is determined in part by the physical setup of the room itself. When it comes to listening to others and speaking in front of others, such physical configurations do make a difference.

As part of your course, be sure to discuss and develop mini-lectures on such topics as the following:

- Ways learners can get help from a professor in a large class
- Special pressures placed on students as speakers when the class size is small
- Differences between the nature of student participation in large lecture halls, small seminars, and more conventionally arranged classrooms
- The impact of alternative seating arrangements on student participation patterns
- What to do if the size of the class or its physical configuration seems uncomfortable

Some Suggestions

Discuss such matters with the class. Ask students to describe what they believe are the most frequent room configurations in mainstream courses. Have them compare how they think the rooms will be arranged with what you know to be the reality on your campus. Bring in photographs of actual classrooms for comparison. Plan for several visits from former ESL students who are already enrolled in mainstream courses. Also arrange for visits from content area course instructors. Ahead of time, ask such visitors to discuss the impacts that alternative class sizes and classroom configurations sometimes have on the dynamics of classroom interactions. Ask them to begin by simply describing the configurations of several different courses they have participated in. They can continue by discussing how these configurations either facilitated or impeded communication from their perspectives.

Design out-of-class survey activities in which your students gather and analyze responses from the general student population on such matters. A series of activities might involve your class in canvassing students to gather firsthand information on class sizes and classroom configurations for mainstream courses they are likely to take in upcoming terms. Ask your students to compare room size, class size, and the physical setup of classrooms across such dimensions as the following: academic discipline, introductory courses, survey courses, lower-division courses, upper-division courses, courses designed for majors in a particular area of study, more advanced courses, seminars, and courses taught by regularly appointed faculty, adjunct faculty, visiting instructors, and graduate teaching assistants.

Draw It Out

Distribute to each student large sheets of flip-chart paper and a few colored pencils or crayons. Ask students to use these materials to draw what they consider to be the typical physical arrangement of mainstream college classrooms. Also ask them to draw an alternative arrangement that might be less common but that they suspect probably does occur. Finally, ask them to draw what they consider to be an ideal classroom arrangement. Once a few drawings are generated, group students together to discuss the advantages and disadvantages of each configuration. How would they feel if asked to speak in front of others in the various types of classroom arrangements depicted in the drawings?

To the extent possible, structure the format for lectures and class discussions in your own course in different ways. Experiment with different options. Sometimes, use a chalk-and-talk format while speaking from the front of the room. At other times, use PowerPoint presentations or a sheet of talking points while seated at a desk. In some classes, address students while seated at the head of a U-shape configuration. On occasion, distribute a partial outline to students as support for making sense of the lecture's content. At other times, deliberately withhold such supports and explain to students that they need to get used to creating complete lecture notes on their own.

Throughout your course planning, keep in mind these issues of class size and spatial configuration of the classroom. Your purpose is to increase learner awareness of the impact such dimensions have on the learning process and on the different roles students must play as speakers in alternative classroom settings. Assist students in learning to adjust their speaking behaviors and other learning strategies to best fit whatever classroom configurations they encounter in a mainstream content area course.

The "Open-U" Configuration

EAP teachers have several options in arranging classroom space to enhance oral communication. In this section, I assume that at times you will want to generate whole-class discussion. Of course, in other lessons—or lesson phases—you might want to avoid a whole-class format and use smaller groups or pair work activities.

When arranging classroom space for a whole-class discussion, it really is an asset if the students' seats are moveable. Some teachers prefer a conventional class arrangement with the teacher's desk at the front and students seated in desks arranged in a large rectangle. Other teachers prefer a large closed circle with everyone facing each other.

In oral communication courses, I find a full-circle format to be somewhat intimidating for learners. Following a brief period of satisfaction with the full circle, both students and teachers begin to complain. A full circle may have the advantage of everyone being able to see everyone else easily, but that is also one of its significant drawbacks. When seated in a full circle, there is nowhere for anyone to hide. Also, at times it is awkward for the teacher to move around the room without calling considerable attention to herself or himself. As an alternative to a full circle format, many teachers prefer the "open-U" configuration. I find that an open U is more conducive to discussion among all those present. To arrange the seats into an open-U formation, proceed as follows.

Setting up the Open U

- Find out local procedures for requesting classroom space on your campus. (At most colleges, rooms are assigned months ahead of time.)
- Take a tour of available classrooms, and locate a few that would serve your needs.
- Well before the start of the term, request a room already set up in a configuration you prefer.

If you are unable to select or renegotiate classroom space, once the course begins you may need to do the following:

- Arrive to class a few minutes early to physically rearrange seats.
- If some students have also arrived early, ask a few to assist you in shifting the furniture in the classroom. If appropriate, ask some of your stronger students to assist you for this purpose.
- For any students who assist you, use this as time to chat with them and get to know them better.
- Arrange (or ask others to assist you in arranging) the seats into an open U so that the space at the front of the room is open with two rows of seats receding to and across the back of the room. The two rows of seats are connected at the back of the room but open at the front.

Teacher seated at the front

- Arrange your own seat within or just slightly in front of the open end of the U at the front of the room. This arrangement will allow you to face the entire class while seated, but it will also allow you to get up and move around the room when you choose to do so. You can move easily around the outside of the U, walk within it, walk behind it, or stay near the front of the room. It is a very flexible arrangement for the teacher and carries many of the advantages of a full-circle format, as well as some additional possibilities.
- In some settings, it is possible to remove extra seats from the room or to place them along a wall (or in the hallway outside the room) so that the teacher and students can move around the room more easily.
- When the class is over (if appropriate), involve a few volunteers to assist you in returning the seats to their original configuration.

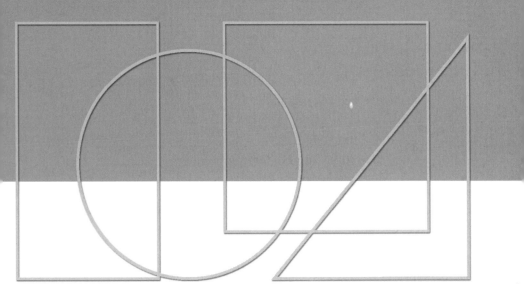

Part **5**

Student Speaking

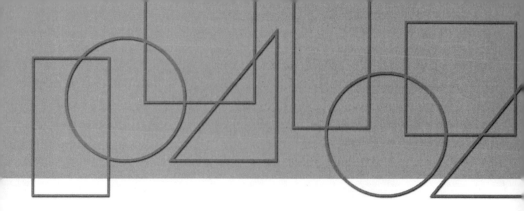

Chapter **12**

Students' Oral Presentations in Class

One of the more difficult challenges ESL learners face is giving an oral presentation from the front of the class. This chapter explores an alternative instructional format. Rather than speak from the front of the room, students work in groups of two. This arrangement provides individual speakers with multiple opportunities to develop and extend their prepared topics while individual listeners practice note-taking skills. The chapter's second half presents a detailed lesson description illustrating this approach. A studio workshop atmosphere develops in the classroom that increases opportunities for discovery, change, and revision in student delivery of oral presentations.

Chapter **13**

Students Need to Know Their Own English Voices

As second language learners, it is essential for students to have a clear sense of what they sound like when speaking English. Of course, it is difficult to gauge how our spoken delivery is perceived by others in any language. Under normal circumstances, when listening to others speak, our ears are picking up sound vibrations that travel through the air around us. But when we hear and listen to our own voices, the sound waves are also passing through the bony and fleshy structures of our heads.

Most of us have experienced the surprise of hearing our own voices for the first time through audio recordings. Many people deny, or at least take some convincing, that they really do "sound like that." The truth is that a clear audio recording played through decent-quality speakers is a reliable record of how our voices really sound to others. Perhaps for the first time, we are hearing our own voices as the sound waves we generate are flowing through the air without passing through the bony and fleshy structures of our heads. Even if we do not like what we hear, such recordings are close to what everyone else hears when we speak.

Beyond the physical sound of one's own voice, there are several important reasons why second language learners should get used to hearing their voices in English. Many issues related to linguistic features of spoken language, such as the pronunciation of individual sounds, sound combinations, word stress, phrase stress, rhythm, intonation, word choice, and syntax, combine to form the distinctive characteristics of one's speech in a second language. Less obvious are such voice features as tempo of delivery, loudness, use of filler words and phrases, emotional tone, and use of pausing patterns to capture listeners' attention.

As ESL learners gain experience communicating with others in English, many become accustomed to listening to the speech styles of native English speakers with whom they interact beyond the classroom. Especially while living in English-dominant parts of the world, models of native English speakers are all around them. But it is difficult for students to learn to self-monitor and compare their own speech patterns with the patterns of native speakers in real time. To progress as language learners in English-medium colleges, the challenge of increasing self-awareness of the quality of one's speech patterns is yet one more challenge EAP learners face. Getting used to the sound of one's own voice in English is another way to facilitate progress in language learning. Encourage learners to continue comparing their own speech patterns with those of competent native English speakers. Do so by providing direct instruction in how to externalize and monitor one's own speech through purposeful use of audio recordings.

What You Can Do

Because the goal for students is to become accustomed to hearing their own speech patterns in English, they need some basic technological tools. The simplest tool is an audio recorder with playback capability. Inexpensive audio recorders can be used both inside and outside the classroom. Ask students to purchase or borrow inexpensive versions of such equipment. They are relatively easy to find. I recently purchased an inexpensive model at a popular discount outlet for under $15.00.

Because digital recorders are a somewhat more expensive option, I find audiocassette recorders to be a good buy. At the start of the courses I teach, I require that students purchase such a recorder if they do not already own one. You can explain that these are basic tools for those who wish to enhance the intelligibility of their speech in English. Key features of whatever machine students purchase are a built-in microphone, recording capability, and playback function. Most machines that have recording capability also have pause capability, which is especially useful for more intensive work in listening to and learning to monitor one's own speech patterns. Ask students to look for recorders with this feature.

Use Class Time to Introduce Relevant Procedures

Students should get into the habit of producing and listening to recordings of themselves speaking in English. At first, they will feel uneasy listening to their own voices, especially in English. You need to get them over these initial stages of doubt. Part of your role is to introduce students to recording procedures so that they can produce recordings of themselves on their own. Set a schedule in which you first introduce the procedures and then discuss options for students to record themselves. For example, some students might prefer to record their speech while reading aloud from written texts of their own selection. Choices include newspaper stories, magazine articles, song lyrics, dialogue excerpts from popular plays, movie screenplays, and scenes from novels. More ambitious students might be interested in recording more extemporaneous conversations with friends, extemporaneous monologues on prepared topics, or their own rehearsals for more formal oral presentations designed to be delivered in academic settings.

Discuss the wide range of options. Solicit suggestions for types of discourse the students would like to record in their own voices. Over time, coax learners to explore alternative types of source material. Discuss advantages and disadvantages of working with fully scripted, semiscripted, and extemporaneous material. Eventually, negotiate a comfortable schedule for students to collect their self-generated materials several times during the semester. Assess students more on their ingenuity in selecting (or generating) material to record and on their conscientiousness in completing required tasks, and not as much on the quality of their actual recorded performances. Celebrate students' successes, and give feedback as possible.

Teach Students How to Work with the Material

Perhaps the easiest and most direct way to have something to say while recording one's own voice is to read aloud from a written script. Virtually any written materials in English can be used. Demonstrate how students can select their own textual material. Discuss the importance of reading the material several times and getting to know it well prior to recording. Show students how they can parse such texts with slash marks and other written conventions to indicate word-, phrase-, and sentence-level stress locations. Involve them in recording segments by speaking into the microphones of their recorders. After they have recorded a brief segment (perhaps only a few sentences), have them stop, rewind, and then listen to themselves reading aloud in English. The object is to work with the recordings and with different kinds of source materials so that learners become ever more familiar with their own voices as they are speaking in English.

Also, demonstrate and discuss with students some of the advantages of working with written texts that are simulations of oral language discourse. For example, text excerpts from movie screenplays (popular dramas work particularly well) or well-known plays such as Neil Simon's *The Odd Couple*, Tennessee Williams's *A Street Car Named Desire*, and Arthur Miller's *Death of a Salesman* are rich sources of scripted language that simulates the nuances of spontaneous speech. Recently, one of my students had located transcripts of the Jerry Seinfeld television show on the Internet (http://www.seinfeldscripts.com/). His recordings of these materials were very effective and entertaining.

Many Internet sites provide free access to screenplays of major motion pictures from the past one hundred years. Having students record their voices as they read such material aloud can be useful for simulating what their voices sound like in less controlled settings. At the time I was working on this chapter, the 2004 Republican and Democratic national conventions had recently taken place. Both political parties provided full transcripts and audio files, free of charge via the Internet, of the major speeches given at the conventions. Students can engage in a lot of productive work (and have fun) with such authentic materials while comparing their own voices and delivery styles to the actual voices and delivery styles of well-known political figures.

Encourage students to be creative in selecting their material. Your purpose is to engage students in a long-term process of generating and listening to recordings they have made of their own English speech patterns.

Once they are comfortable with generating the recordings, move on to more ambitious stages of teaching the kinds of speech features to listen for.

The point is to have students eventually generate recordings of their extemporaneous speech in English. I find it best for students to record such speech samples in private. Spend time in class having students brainstorm lists of topics they could talk about extemporaneously. Often, the time you spend in class brainstorming possible topics to talk about will motivate students to make higher-quality recordings on their own. Once students have produced recordings of their own voices, teach them how to use the recordings to analyze their own and each other's speech patterns. Features to attend to on alternative listenings to the same recordings include the following:

- Tempo of delivery
- Pausing patterns
- Articulation of word endings (especially of important content nouns and verbs)
- Rhythm at sentence level
- Word-level stress
- Control of syntax
- Blendings between words within phrases
- Vowel enunciations that fall on stressed syllables of important content words
- Control over vocal emphasis to call listener attention to key ideas and important ideas

Involve students in deciding how they want to work with recorded samples of their own speech. Your primary objective is to introduce procedures for EAP students to learn to monitor their own speech so that they continue to develop along the interlanguage continuum. Ideally, they will continue to explore such options for autonomous learning long after the course is over.

Chapter **14**

Extending Length of Speaking Turns

Time spent in the classroom will never be enough. One of your more important roles is to encourage learners to use their time beyond the classroom efficiently. This chapter introduces ways of increasing learners' abilities as speakers through both in-class and out-of-class speaking opportunities. Relative length of speaking turns is a prominent characteristic of speech performance. Although shorter speaking turns work well in many settings, the demands of academic communication push learners to speak for longer periods of time. When speaking up to make a point during class, for example, an ESL student may need to maintain the floor for several minutes. Along with other related topics, in this chapter you will learn ways of teaching students to lengthen their speaking turns.

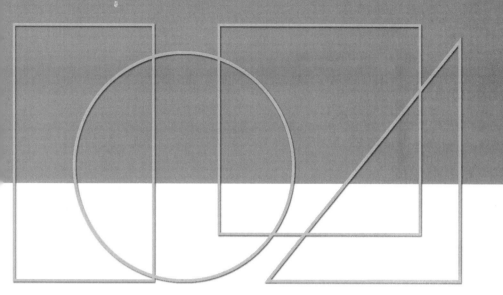

Part **6**

Vocabulary and Speech Intelligibility

Chapter **15**

Specialized Vocabulary and Polysyllabic Words

FEATURED IN THIS CHAPTER

- How vocabulary supports development of speaking-to-learn abilities
- Polysyllabic words and academic vocabulary
- Why word-level stress is an important concern
- Tools for focusing on word-level stress
- How to identify primary-stress syllables

An essential part of the spoken language that students will use in university classrooms is a specialized form of vocabulary. College classrooms are places where technical, specialized, and polysyllabic words are more common than in nonacademic settings. This is an area where differences between social and academic uses of spoken English are easy to recognize. Although we do not use words such as *ambiguous, phenomenon, notwithstanding,* and *category* very often in everyday speech, we would not be surprised to find these kinds of words used frequently in college classrooms. These dimensions of vocabulary usage are relevant to the teaching of EAP speaking-to-learn abilities because both teachers and students need academic words to get their ideas across in class. Students need them for study purposes, as well. The issue is not only that students must be able to recognize such words when they hear them, but also that discourse conventions in college classrooms compel students to use such words.

How can we initiate the process of helping students begin to recognize and use academic words? Let's begin with the stages of building awareness. One of your challenges is to build learner awareness of the important role such words play. Talk with students about academic vocabulary words. Remind them that modern English has a long history of development from Latin, Greek, German, French, and other languages. Many academic words have roots in these languages, especially Latin and French. Many such words are less commonly used outside academic settings.

To initiate the process of building awareness, I find it useful to send students on scavenger hunts tied to whatever written materials are used in the course. Their task is to generate a list of academic words appearing in our course materials, the kinds of words they normally would not encounter in casual conversations with their friends. Once they can work with their EAP course materials in this way, extend similar activities to other types of materials. These include textbooks from other content area courses, library resources, and other resources tied to the disciplines they are considering as majors. A significant activity tied to the words brought back to class is to discuss them interactively so that students grow accustomed to hearing the words they identify and to using them productively in their speech.

When the assigned task is to search for words to bring to class, teach students how to use effectively the kinds of textual supports commonly featured in college textbooks. Remind students that textbooks are structured deliberately to call attention to the kinds of words that are useful to start using in an EAP class. The textual supports I have in mind include glossaries, indexes, and tables of contents, as well as the use of bold print, underlining, italics, alternative colors, and different fonts within individual chapters. Such text features are common in textbooks and can be exploited productively so that students discover for themselves some of the core academic vocabulary of their future areas of study. In sum, part of your role is to involve students in gathering and sharing their own examples of academic words from selected disciplines.

Beyond building awareness of such vocabulary, also set up classroom tasks that will prepare students to begin using academic words. Fortunately, several Internet sites provide lists of specialized words featured in university classrooms. I find it useful to introduce students to the Academic Word List (AWL) as made available at the following Internet site by Averil Coxhead,[1] one of the authors of the Houghton Mifflin series: http://www.vuw.ac.nz/lals/research/awl/.

As students bring in their own words, identify other academic words to focus on. It is essential to find ways to incorporate them into the normal routine of in-class discussion. The next chapter introduces some ideas for getting students to focus their attention on the pronunciation of new words while using them during interactive classroom activities.

Attending to Word-Level Stress

When starting to use a new word, an EAP student is entering a process of really learning it and of allowing it to reach deep into memory structures. That is, the student is more likely to access the new word from memory as needed, to recognize it while reading or listening to others, and to use it with increasing confidence as a speaker. To really "know a word," EAP learners must become familiar with the word's form (spoken, written, and word parts), meaning, and use. All three dimensions are essential to expanding vocabulary knowledge and spoken control over recently acquired words. When we teach speaking-to-learn abilities, we should call special attention to the spoken forms of new words while also ensuring that learners understand word meanings and can use new words appropriately in a range of settings, but especially in classrooms.

It is important to coach learners into starting to use new words. The academic experience includes challenging speaking experiences in which students participate in study groups, ask questions in class, respond to instructor and peers, make in-class reports, visit instructors during office hours, and leave coherent voice mail messages. Speaking up and attempting to use new words are important parts of the vocabulary acquisition process. To feel confident at such times, students need at least a threshold level of intelligibility in connection with the new words they are trying to use.

Having intelligible control over the spoken form of recently acquired vocabulary and vocabulary still in the process of being acquired is one of the significant challenges EAP learners face.

Why do I include the image of students starting to use new words they are still in the process of acquiring? Learners depend on multiple exposures to a new word, as well as on multiple opportunities to use a new word, before they can gain anything close to confident control over a word's usage and meaning. Using new words while speaking is an integral part of both acquiring vocabulary and mastering course content. In connection with a word's spoken form, teachers and learners should keep two primary concerns in mind: (1) What does the target word sound like, and (2) how is it pronounced? Do not expect EAP speakers to remember and know how to use new academic words without special training in this area.

In addition to increasing vocabulary knowledge, there is another reason for encouraging learners to start using the new vocabulary that surrounds them. It has to do with connections between the stress patterns of individual words and the rhythm of spoken language. In mainstream courses, use of academic words is much greater than in nonacademic situations. The types of academic words I refer to are infrequently used in most social situations. Such words may be of Latin or French origin, and many are polysyllabic with up to six syllables. When polysyllabic words are spoken in English, they manifest alternating stressed and unstressed syllables that serve as building blocks for distinctive rhythmic patterns. When these patterns are produced by English speakers, they act as signals for listeners to recognize the syllabic structure of incoming words and intended meanings.

Attending to stress and rhythm patterns at the level of individual words provides a wonderful opportunity to prepare learners for the important ways in which stress, rhythm, and even intonation function across broad stretches of spoken language. Basic principles of how stress and rhythm operate at word level can later be extended across phrase, sentence, and broader discourse levels. For example, the academic word *perspective* carries a stress pattern that is essentially the same as the stress pattern for the phrase "How ARE you?" Try saying them for yourself: "perSPECtive" / "How ARE you?" Both take essentially the same amount of time to produce, and both have an especially prominent second syllable.

Likewise, stress patterns are parallel in the word *economical* and in an unmarked production of the phrase "We can GET you there." Without altering how each might be said in a normal conversation, how similar do their stress patterns sound to you? "ecoNOMical" / "We can GET you there." Each utterance has five syllables with primary stress on the third syllable. The point is a potentially important one. Attention to word-level stress of academic words can serve as an entry into the teaching of even more general rhythmic patterns of spoken English beyond the level of individual words.

In the classroom, how can you interest learners in paying close attention to the pronunciation, including the stress and rhythm patterns, of academic words? When working with EAP learners, it is important to keep things simple to facilitate useful classroom routines. Introduce some easily recognized principles and strategies. The following are some straightforward procedures you can use to call learners' attention to word-level stress patterns of new vocabulary words. Many teachers have found the procedures especially useful when working with EAP learners. They can be adapted, however, and applied when working with students learning English for other purposes.[2]

1. As learners encounter new words, remind them of two basic questions while focusing on word-level stress patterns: What does the word sound like, and how is the word pronounced? As they focus on an individual word, ask them to work their way through the following additional steps.

2. Identify the number of syllables. Ask yourself, how many syllables does the word have? As preliminary groundwork, learners need practice in learning what syllables are and how to count them. Plan to show students how to use the pronunciation keys of good dictionaries to tally syllables. If learners are unsure of a word's total number of syllables, ask them to get into the habit of checking in a dictionary. Also encourage them to listen carefully after they have asked a native or near-native English speaker to say or use the word.

3. Tap it out. Have students tap lightly against the top of their desks as they count each of the word's syllables in succession. Alternatively, students could clap their hands or tap their feet, but it is important that the number of syllables and the word's overall rhythm be signaled by some sort of physical gesture.

4. Where is the strongest syllable? Which syllable is the strongest when an English speaker says the word? As students continue to tap out the word, be sure they tap a bit harder on this specific syllable. This is a rhythmic feature.
5. If unsure, repeat steps 2 and 3.
6. Is there another strong syllable? If there is, keep this one in mind, too.
7. Use a numeric code. Eventually, it will be useful to ask students to label the word with either a two-digit (or, if needed, a three-digit) numeric system that illustrates the following conventions. (See Figure 15.1.) The first digit represents the word's total number of syllables. The second digit represents the location of the word's primary stressed syllable. If needed, a third digit may be added to represent the location of a secondary stressed syllable.

    For example, a frequent pattern of word-level stress is that many words of three syllables carry primary stress on the second syllable (e.g., *perspective, discussion, approaches*). I suggest you refer to this as the basic "3-2" pattern. That is, the initial number 3 indicates that each of these words has three syllables; the number 2 following the hyphen signals that primary stress falls on each of the words' second syllables. Once you have determined how many syllables a target word has and location of its primary stressed syllable, you and your students can use the numeric system as shorthand for categorizing and discussing the stress pattern of individual words. Although the word *perspective* may be classified as a 3-2 word, this system characterizes a word such as *interpersonal* as a 5-3-1 word. For the word *interpersonal,* the inclusion of a third digit in the word's numeric description signals (a) the presence and (b) the location of a secondary stressed syllable. That is, the descriptor 5-3-1 signals that (a) *interpersonal* is a five-syllable word (the number 5 is the descriptor's initial digit), (b) primary stress falls on its third syllable (the number 3 is the descriptor's second digit), (c) there is a secondary stress (the appearance of a third digit in the descriptor), and (d) the location of this word's secondary stressed syllable coincides with its first syllable (the numeric value of the descriptor's third digit).

    For even more advanced work, you sometimes must acknowledge that some words in English have more than a single secondary stressed syllable. To illustrate, in a more advanced proficiency class you might begin the characterization of a word such as *methodology* by referring to it as a 5-3 word (five syllables with primary stress on the third syllable). To make the word's characterization more complete, you need conventions to indicate that this 5-3 word carries secondary stresses on both its first and final syllables. To signal this additional information, classify *methodology* as a 5-3-_1-5_ word. In this case, the last two digits (that is, the 1-5 sequence) would be used to signal the locations of secondary stress on both its first and fifth syllables. In the 5-3-1-5 code, the final 1-5 section follows the nature order of the word (the sequence of the 1 coming before 5 does not denote anything about relative degree of secondary stress).

As part of recurring classroom activities when working with new vocabulary, examine individual words in connection with (a) total number of syllables, (b) the location of each word's primary stressed syllable, and (c) the location of any secondary stressed syllable(s).

8. Tap out the word with some sort of a physical gesture while making the strongest syllable obvious.

The following is a visual depiction of numeric conventions for identifying stress patterns in words featured in a content area recently assigned to students. The vocabulary words are taken from the topic area of the communication process.

Numeric Conventions To Identify Stress Patterns		
Vocabulary Word	**Stress Pattern**	**What It Means**
purpose	2-1	2-syllable word primary stress on 1st syllable
assert	2-2	2-syllable word primary stress on 2nd syllable
attention	3-2	3-syllable word primary stress on 2nd syllable
advertise	3-1 (or 3-1-3)	3-syllable word primary stress on 1st syllable (secondary stress on 3rd syllable)
participants	4-2 (or 4-2-1)	4-syllable word primary stress on the 2nd syllable (secondary stress on 1st syllable)
nationality	5-3 (or 5-3-1)	5-syllable word primary stress on the 3rd syllable (secondary stress on 1st syllable)

If students are unable to complete any of the steps outlined above or if they have trouble with steps 2, 4, 6, or 8, for example, they have several options. They may work with the pronunciation key of a dictionary. They can ask their teacher or some other competent English speaker to say the word as they listen carefully. When all else fails, I like to engage a student in a one-on-one exchange in which as the teacher I use the word several times in the context of whole sentences while the student listens and tries to figure out the pattern by ear. Another option available to students is to make an informed guess by applying some of the word analysis skills you can feature in the course for determining the location of primary stressed syllables. The following are practice activities tied to some of the teaching strategies and the numbering system presented thus far. The practice activities were designed by Cheryl Delk (2004),[3] an author of one of the EAP oral communication course texts of the Houghton Mifflin Series.

Task 1

Listening and Speaking Strategy:
Numbering Syllables and Stress in New Words

In this course, we are using a numbering system to identify the number of syllables and the strongest syllable in words. In each English word, there is one syllable that is the longest, loudest, and highest in pitch. Recognizing that syllable, both in speaking and in listening, is important for effective communication.

Here's an example. Listen to your instructor pronounce the word *device*:

de • vice´

We can see that this word has two syllables and the stress is on the second syllable. Tap your fingers twice on the table as you say "device." Tap and pronounce the word again, putting extra stress on the second syllable.

An easy way for remembering how to pronounce this word is writing the number of syllables, and then the number of the stressed syllable, with a dash (–) between these two numbers. For example, for *device* we would write "2-2", meaning that the word has two syllables and the second syllable is stressed.

Listen to your instructor pronounce the word *illuminate*:

il • lu´ • mi • nate

Tap your fingers four times on the table as you hear the word. Tap and pronounce the word, putting stress on the second syllable. We can identify this word as a "4-2 word."

Task 2

**Learning the Pronunciation of Your New Words:
Syllables and Stress**

Listen to the pronunciation of these words. Use the numbering system to indicate how many syllables there are in each word and which syllable is stressed. Then, practice pronouncing these words out loud with a partner.

1. patent   (_____ - _____)
2. accompany   (_____ - _____)
3. advance   (_____ - _____)
4. initial   (_____ - _____)
5. envision   (_____ - _____)
6. simultaneous (_____ - _____)
7. makeshift   (_____ - _____)
8. acquire   (_____ - _____)

The numeric conventions for analyzing stress patterns of academic words are one characteristic feature of the oral communication course texts of the series. In the series, you will find numerous activities centered on these teaching procedures. Even if you do not work with one of these course texts, many EAP learners find the teaching strategies I introduce in this chapter to be helpful.

Endnotes

1. Coxhead, A. 2000. A new academic word list. *TESOL Quarterly, 34*(2), 213–238.
2. The eight-step strategies for identifying primary stress locations of polysyllabic words first appeared in: Murphy, J. M. 2004. Attending to word-stress while learning new vocabulary. *English for Specific Purposes Journal, 23*(1), 67–83.
3. Task 1 and Task 2 from Cheryl Delk, "Try This in Your Next Class!," *Houghton Mifflin Academic Success Newsletter, 1*(2), 4–5. Reprinted by permission of Houghton Mifflin Company.

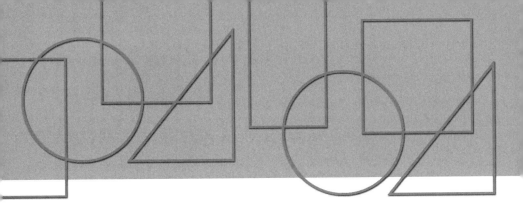

Chapter **16**

Give Some Attention to Vowels and Final Consonants

Once students have grasped the importance of using specialized academic vocabulary, it is essential to provide them with a range of ways to continue using such words in extemporaneous speech. Building upon Chapter 15, which highlighted features of stress and rhythms patterns in academic vocabulary, this chapter introduces ways to build learner awareness of the more prominent vowel and consonant sounds featured in the academic words students are learning to use. The idea is to avoid overemphasizing the role that sound segments play while giving them appropriate and accessible degrees of attention. Assisting learners in learning to work efficiently with vowel and consonant sounds is yet another way of getting them to think about and use specialized academic vocabulary. The several tools introduced in the chapter are highly practical and focused on what learners really need to know in order to be intelligible speakers in academic settings.

Part 7

Ongoing Professional Concerns

Adopt the Attitude of an Exploratory Teacher

- What does it mean to be an exploratory teacher?
- How to identify and learn about the "action zone" of your class
- Gathering formative feedback from students on how you are doing
- The importance of being a team player

All teachers have room to grow. All of us experience uneasy moments as part of the teaching process and sometimes encounter puzzling events during our interactions with language learners. These are normal parts of teachers' lives. If we are to stay alive and vital as language teachers, we must adopt the attitude of the inquisitive teacher-explorer (an explorer of teaching and of student learning): be continually interested in learning more about teaching and learning processes. As we become exploratory teachers, the purposes of our explorations are to (a) expand our understanding of the teaching-learning process, (b) expand our repertoire of strategic options as language teachers, and (c) enhance the quality of the learning opportunities we provide to learners in language classrooms. To these ends, we can deepen awareness of teaching and learning behaviors by working to improve our abilities to:

- Gather information on whatever is taking place within the language classroom
- Examine such information closely to better understand just what is going on
- Identify anything puzzling about the teaching-learning process that may intrigue us
- Build awareness and deepen understanding of current teaching and learning behaviors
- Locate and collaborate with others interested in the processes of exploratory teaching and the enhancement of language learning
- Pose and refine questions tied to our own teaching that are worth further exploration
- Locate resources that may help clarify whatever questions are being posed and/or puzzles being encountered
- Make informed changes in teaching, even if they are only modest changes
- Document changes in teaching-learning behaviors and responses
- Continue such efforts over time and share emerging insights with others

The Exploratory Teacher

To examine your classroom as an exploratory teacher, you first need to realize that each language course is unique. As are all instances of language teaching, the teaching of EAP oral communication is part of a complex process of interactions between and among all those present in the room. A first step in exploring the complexity of your classroom is to acknowledge this complexity and focus your attention on the course as it is unfolding.

General topic areas that teachers often explore include (a) communication patterns in the classroom, (b) decision making as the classroom teacher, (c) ways learners apply knowledge, (d) the affective climate of the classroom, (e) the instructional environment, and (f) self-assessment of growth and development as a professional. Chapter 18 highlights resources for learning more about processes of exploratory teaching.

Identify the "Action Zone" of Your Class

After a short time teaching a new course, you will notice emerging patterns of learner participation. In most classes, it is common for the same few class members to volunteer responses to the teacher's questions and other types of whole-class solicits. A normal tendency in language classrooms is for some students to be more participatory and more outgoing than others. At the opposite extreme, a few students may rarely respond to questions directed to the whole group. Those more vocal students in class constitute what is sometimes called the *action zone*. One of your challenges is to try to reach as many members of the class as possible. The idea is to take deliberate steps to include as many students as possible in the action zone.

Steps in Identifying the Class Action Zone

Take stock of the status quo in your class. Be honest with yourself and with the members of the class. No language class is perfect, and student participation patterns in the classroom will never be perfect. Even if unintentional, you may favor some students. Likewise, some students may be more responsive and receptive to your teaching style than others. In comparison with other members of the class, some students may tend to have more to contribute because of personality, learning style, ability in English, degree of affinity with you as the teacher, or some other factors. Such differences between students are normal parts of the teaching process. However, teachers are in a prime position to do something about the status quo.

It is important to gather information on communication patterns. Usually it is not enough to rely on your memory when identifying such patterns in your classroom. Because you are such an integral member of the teaching process, it is difficult, without some sort of outside support and perspective, for you to assess what is happening. Yet part of your challenge is to figure out what is taking place. Some options to try in identifying which members of the class constitute the action zone:

- Keep a running tally of student participation live, during the lesson.
- Invite a visitor, an experienced teacher, to observe the class.
- Videotape a few lessons.
- Audiotape a few lessons.
- Keep a retrospective teaching journal of who participates during lessons.
- Keep mental track of such patterns as you teach.

Chart the communication patterns. Personally, I prefer to videotape a few lessons for such purposes, although the option of working with a visitor-observer can be effective, as well. With the support of a video recording or an observer's notes, it is relatively straightforward to identify the more participatory members of the class. If time permits, tally the number of responses from individual students and rank order the degrees and sequencing of their participation.

Identify the members of the action zone. Even taking the initial step of knowing who the members of the action zone are is often enough to make a difference. You are more likely to reach other students if you are better informed on who those in need of more support might be.

Develop a plan to add others to the action zone. You can begin to reach out to the less participatory students in many ways. Minimally, keep a list of their names on the front desk, or use an identifier such as highlighted names on the class roster. Another possibility is to keep a stack of index cards, one card for each student. During phases of instructor-fronted teaching, work with the cards to be sure you call on as many members of the class as you can. Use such visual supports to (a) increase the number of times you call on those who have been less participatory and (b) design activities specifically geared to the strengths of those members of the class.

Continue to revisit this topic periodically during the course. Action zones may change unexpectedly. These are ongoing and evolving features of language classrooms. It is useful to revisit the changing nature of such patterns every few weeks.

Formative Feedback to You from Students

A direct way for learning more about learners' perceptions of your efforts as their teacher is to ask them. To gather more useful feedback from students, however, the challenge is to find a way that keeps their comments anonymous. One procedure that EAP students respond particularly well to is called *"five-minute" papers*. This procedure provides opportunities for students to voice their concerns. Of course, it can be overdone. I suggest that five-minute papers be used no more than once a week, although once every two weeks is a viable alternative.

The procedure is as follows. A few minutes before the end of the selected lesson, announce that you want to give students a chance to provide feedback on how things are going in the course. Explain that your purposes are to gather formative feedback and to make any necessary changes in how you offer the course. Tell students that they will be given five minutes to write their comments. Explain that you will not read their comments yourself but that, instead, you will leave their comments with a colleague. This colleague is the person who will read their five-minute papers. Assure the class that, later, you and your colleague will have a friendly conversation in which the colleague reveals to you the gist of what the class members said.

It is a good idea to emphasize that collaborating with a colleague ensures anonymity. In this way, not even their handwriting will reveal the writers of particular comments. To go a step further, you could arrange for one of the students to pass the class's five-minute papers to your colleague.

Once students understand the procedures you have planned, ask everyone to take out a sheet of paper and to write responses to a very general prompt such as, "How are things going for you in the course? Is there anything you would like me to handle differently? Would you like to see any changes in the course?" I usually display the writing prompt as an overhead projection generated prior to class. After you have presented the prompt, leave enough time for students to compose responses. Although I call it a five-minute paper, some students may need a bit more time than that to express what they want to say. Start early enough to give them enough time. On other days, alternate other kinds of writing prompts for five-minute papers. Here are some examples that I might use on separate days:

- What is the one thing you are likely to remember from today's class?
- What was the most confusing concept we covered?
- Is there anything you would like to know more about?
- Is there anything you think I should be doing differently?
- Do you have any suggestions for improving the course?
- Does the course textbook seem helpful?
- What characteristics of the teacher's instructional style work well?
- What characteristics of the teacher's instructional style do you find to be less helpful?

Learners' responses to such questions are especially useful when you assure anonymity and explain that the purpose of five-minute papers is to give you some direction on changes that might be needed in the course. Although five-minute papers take time away from the regular lesson, using them can have a constructive impact on subsequent teaching decisions. Invariably, I find something of value in what students have to say. Using the papers wisely can remind students that their responses to the course are valued and given serious attention.

Language Teachers Are Team Players

Teaching does not take place in a vacuum. You are part of a wider language teaching program, and your colleagues depend on your contributions to the larger group. The focus of this final section is how to build a reputation as a team player. This may seem an odd topic in a book titled *Essentials of Teaching Academic Oral Communication*. The fact is, though, that if you fail to be an effective team player in the language program where you work, the quality of learning opportunities you will be able to provide to learners will suffer. In fact, if you do not learn to be a team player, you will not be around as a teacher very long.

We live in an era of interconnectivity in which the members of most professions, including the language teaching profession, function as a team. Some of the strongest complaints voiced by directors/administrators of language programs concern classroom teachers who behave as if their work takes place in isolation from their colleagues and the wider program.

Nothing could be further from the truth. Without belaboring a discussion of the ongoing administrative tasks that must be addressed and completed in a successful language program, suffice it to say that administrators' and other teachers' tasks and responsibilities are considerable. All your colleagues depend on you and the entire faculty's support to keep things running smoothly.

Wherever you teach, in whatever kind of language program, you must think and behave as a team player. For example, there will always be meetings to attend and responsibilities to meet that may seem only loosely related to the courses you offer. All of us realize the difficulties in making the time necessary to attend what we may perceive as meetings dedicated to not much more than administrative topics. Bear in mind that we all face such difficulties, teachers and administrators alike. But to build a reputation as a team player, you must not only attend such meetings but also go beyond minimal expectations:

- Arrive on time.
- Stay for the entire meeting.
- Contribute to discussion as appropriate.
- Avoid any impulse to dominate discussion.
- Be accommodating to others as appropriate.
- Speak your mind cordially when needed.
- Serve as a facilitator of discussion when needed.
- Volunteer your services when tasks need to be completed.
- Follow through on agreed-upon responsibilities.

E-mail communications are a basic operating procedure in virtually all North American language programs. Knowing how to use e-mail, however, is not enough. You must also develop habits of good e-mail etiquette. If this is a new topic for you, use an Internet search engine to locate discussions on e-mail etiquette or, as it is better known, "netiquette," to learn some fundamental principles. The following Internet site is useful for such purposes: http://www.onlinenetiquette.com/courtesy1.html.

Examples of netiquette rules.

- Do not type in all capital letters.
- Never give out phone numbers or other personal information.
- When replying to e-mails, always respond promptly and edit out unnecessary information from the post you are responding to.
- If you receive a nasty e-mail, do not respond immediately—if at all.

- Always end your e-mails with "Thank you," "Sincerely," "Take it easy," "Best regards"—something!
- Keep in mind that all private e-mail is considered copyrighted by the original author.
- Always minimize, compress, or "zip" large files before sending them.
- Never send anyone an e-mail about anything if he or she did not specifically request that information from you.

Minimally, get into the habits of reviewing your messages regularly and responding to e-mail messages promptly. In ways parallel to the use of e-mail, develop responsible ways of leaving and responding to voice mail messages, as well as of responding to memos and more personal communications.

In addition to behaviors while attending meetings and staying connected through administrative and other communications, there are many facets to the role you play as a colleague-teacher and member of a language program. Demonstrate to others that you are well organized, conscientious, and capable of being a leader. Develop the reputation of being a team player, especially by being responsive to administrative concerns. Do your best to learn about the program overall, including the content and format of other courses students are taking.

Chapter **18**

Where to Go to Learn More

Throughout this book, I have called attention to resources for learning more about topics featured in particular chapters. In this final chapter, I offer additional suggestions on where to turn to continue your exploration of themes and topics featured in Chapters 1 through 17.

In the next section, I place full citation references beneath specific topic headings that are arranged according to common themes. Within each group, the works cited are not presented in alphabetical order. Rather, I present them in rank order according to my personal preferences. The first items within each group are discussions I consider priorities for anyone teaching oral communication for academic purposes. Likewise, the first topic headings seem especially important, as well.

Some readings appear under more than one heading. A reading's first mention carries its full citation information. If mentioned again, I include only the author's name and date of publication. The various headings and the citations under those headings are arranged according to the priorities a teacher might face when first assigned to teach a course in speaking and listening for academic purposes. In other words, the more essential headings appear first. The headings and citation arrangements within each group reflect my own preferences and understanding of available literature. Because all of us have our own histories and preferences as language teachers, I encourage you to examine the list of resources with a critical eye.

If you are reading this book from the perspective of a current or prospective teacher of academic oral communication, you are in for many rewarding teaching experiences. EAP listening-to-learn and speaking-to-learn specialist literatures are fascinating, if only just beginning, and students really do need your support. EAP learners are terrific to work with.

If you will indulge me for a moment, I would like to end this discussion with a plea. The innovations you are sure to make while teaching oral communication for academic purposes will be of great interest to other EAP teachers. Our field is in need of teachers like you who are gaining classroom experience in this area. As your experience teaching in this area accumulates, consider sharing with others the innovations and improvements you incorporate into your courses. Use such forums as departmental meetings; committee work; local, regional, and international conference presentations; newsletter articles; and journal submissions. If you are new to the field and these kinds of professional activities may seem daunting, good places to begin are within your local setting (e.g., the program you work in, local conferences). With time, some of the other forums mentioned will feel more accessible. Wherever you decide to begin, your contributions will be greatly appreciated by those who learn about your work. These are some of the ways we all move forward as teachers interested in developing students' academic oral communication abilities.

Items to Read Right Away

- Ferris, D., & Tagg, T. (1996a). Academic oral communication needs of EAP learners: What subject-matter instructors actually require. *TESOL Quarterly, 30*(1), 31–58.
- Ferris, D., & Tagg, T. (1996b). Academic listening/speaking tasks for ESL students: Problems, suggestions, and implications. *TESOL Quarterly, 30*(2), 297–320.
- Mendelsohn, D. (1992). Making the speaking class a real learning experience: The keys to teaching spoken English. *TESOL Canada Journal, 10*(1), 72–89.
- Murphy, J. M. (1991). Oral communication in TESOL: Integrating speaking, listening, and pronunciation. *TESOL Quarterly, 25*(2), 51–76.

General Methods Discussions

- Brown, H. D. (2001a). *Teaching by principles: An interactive approach to language pedagogy.* Prentice-Hall: Englewood Cliffs, NJ.
- Celce-Murcia, M. (Ed.). (2001). *Teaching English as a second or foreign language* (2nd ed.). Boston: Heinle & Heinle.
- Stoller, F., & Grabe, W. (1997). A six-T's approach to content-based instruction (Chap. 6, pp. 78–94). In M. Snow & D. Brinton (Eds.), *The content-based classroom: Perspectives on integrating language and content.* Addison Wesley Longman: White Plains, NY.
- Murphy, J. M., & Byrd, H. P. (Eds.). (2001). *Understanding the courses we teach: Local perspectives on English language teaching.* Ann Arbor: University of Michigan Press. [Particularly, chapters 4 and 5 on overall course design]

EAP Speaking and Listening Needs

- Ferris, D., & Tagg, T. (1996a).
- Ferris, D., & Tagg, T. (1996b).
- Chaudron, C. (1995). Academic listening. In D. J. Mendelsohn & J. Rubin (Eds.), *A guide for the teaching of listening* (pp. 74–96). San Diego, CA: Dominie Press.
- Horowitz, D. M. (1986). What professors actually require: Academic tasks for the ESL classroom. *TESOL Quarterly, 20,* 445–462.

Teaching Oral Communication

- Brown, H. D. (2001b). Teaching oral communication skills (Chap. 17, pp. 267–295). In *Teaching by principles: An interactive approach to language pedagogy.* New York: Longman.
- Bailey, K. M., & Savage, L. (1994). *New ways in teaching speaking.* Alexandria, VA: TESOL. [An activities recipe collection]
- Nunan, D., & Miller, L. (1995). *New ways in teaching listening.* Alexandria, VA: TESOL International. [An activities recipe collection]

Assessment

- Mendelsohn, D. J. (1991/92). Instruments for feedback in oral communication. *TESOL Journal, 1*(2), 25–30.

Academic Listening

- Chaudron, C. (1995).
- Murphy, J. M. (1996). Integrating listening and reading instruction in English for academic purposes (EAP) programs. *English for Specific Purposes, 15*(2), 105–120.
- Mendelsohn, D. J. (1994). *Learning to listen: A strategy-based approach for the teaching of listening comprehension.* San Diego, CA: Dominie Press.
- Flowerdew, J. (1994). *Academic listening: Research perspectives.* New York: Cambridge University Press.
- Mendelsohn, D. J., & Rubin. J. (Eds.), *A guide for the teaching of listening.* San Diego, CA: Dominie Press.

Contrastive Analysis between Spoken Forms of English and Other Languages

- Swan, M., & Smith, B. (2001). *Learner English: A teacher's guide to interference and other problems* (2nd ed., *Cambridge Handbooks for Language Teachers*). Cambridge, UK: Cambridge University Press.
- Avery, P., & Ehrlich, S. (1992). The identification and correction of specific pronunciation problems. In P. Avery & S. Ehrlich (Eds.), *Teaching American English pronunciation* (Part II, pp. 93–160). New York: Oxford University Press.

Teaching Academic Vocabulary

- Coxhead, A. (2000). A new academic word list. *TESOL Quarterly, 34*(2), 213–238. [Also on the Internet, go to http://www.vuw.ac.nz/lals/research/awl/]
- Nation, P. (2001). *Learning vocabulary in another language.* Cambridge, UK: Cambridge University Press.

Focus on Pronunciation

- Celce-Murcia, M., Brinton, D., & Goodwin, J. (1996). *Teaching pronunciation: A reference for teachers of English to speakers of other languages.* New York: Cambridge University Press.
- Murphy, J. M. (1996). Teaching pronunciation dramatically: Using excerpts from plays. In V. Whiteson (Ed.), *New ways of using drama and literature in language teaching* (pp. 119–122). Alexandria, VA: TESOL.
- Morley, J. (1994). Multidimensional curriculum design for speech-pronunciation instruction. In J. Morley (Ed.), *Pronunciation pedagogy and theory: New views, new directions* (pp. 64–91). Alexandria, VA: TESOL.

Stress and Rhythm

- Murphy, J. M. (2004). Attending to word-stress while learning new vocabulary. *English for Specific Purposes Journal, 23*(1), 67–83. [On the Internet, open the following DOI site with your browser: http://dx.doi.org, then enter the following DOI citation: 10.1016/S0889-4906(03)00019-X, and finally click Go.]

- Murphy, J. M., & Kandil, M. (2004). Word-level stress patterns in the academic word list. *System: An International Journal of Educational Technology and Applied Linguistics, 32*(1), 61–74. [On the Internet, open the following DOI site with your browser: http://dx.doi.org, then enter the DOI citation 10.1016/j.system.2003.06.001, and finally click Go.]
- Murphy, J. M. (1994). Introducing vowel symbols through information-gap procedures. In K. M. Bailey (Ed.), *New ways in teaching speaking* (pp. 233–240). Washington, DC: TESOL.
- Delk, C. (2004). Try this in your next class! *Houghton Mifflin Academic Success Newsletter, 1*(2), 4–5.
- Acton, W. (2001). FocalSpeak: Integrating rhythm and stress in speech-pronunciation, In J. M. Murphy & H. P. Byrd (Eds.), *Understanding the courses we teach: Local perspectives on English language teaching* (pp. 197–217). Ann Arbor: University of Michigan Press.
- Acton, W. (1984). Changing fossilized pronunciation. *TESOL Quarterly, 18*(1), 71–86.

Students' Oral Presentations: Focus on Dyads

- Murphy, J. M. (1992). Preparing ESL students for the basic speech course: Approach, design, and procedure. *English for Specific Purposes, 11*(1), 51–70.
- Murphey, T. (2001). Videoing conversations for self-evaluation in Japan. In J. M. Murphy & H. P. Byrd (Eds.), *Understanding the courses we teach: Local perspectives on English language teaching* (pp. 179–196). Ann Arbor: University of Michigan Press.
- Murphey, T., & Kenny, T. (1998). Videoing conversations for self-evaluation. *Japan Association of Language Teaching Journal, 20*(1), 126–140.

Bloom's Taxonomy of Question Types

- Bloom, B. S. (Ed.). (1956). *Taxonomy of educational objectives: The classification of educational goals: Handbook I, cognitive domain.* New York: Longman.

Length of Speaking Turns

- Graham, J. G., & Barone, S. M. (2001). Academic speaking: Learning to take "longer turns." In J. M. Murphy & H. P. Byrd (Eds.), *Understanding the courses we teach: Local perspectives on English language teaching* (pp. 409–428). Ann Arbor: University of Michigan Press.
- Brown, G. B., & Yule, G. (1983). *Teaching the spoken language: An approach based on the analysis of conversational English.* Cambridge, UK: Cambridge University Press.

Exploratory Teaching

- Allwright, D., & Bailey, K. (1991). *Focus on the language classroom: An introduction to classroom research for language teachers.* New York: Cambridge University Press.
- Gebhard, J., & Oprandy, R. (1999). *Language teaching awareness: A guide to exploring beliefs and practices.* New York: Cambridge University Press.
- Murphy, J. M. (2001). Reflective teaching in English language teaching. In M. Celce-Murcia (Ed.), *Teaching English as a second or foreign language* (3rd ed., pp. 499–515). Boston: Heinle & Heinle.
- Richards, J. C., & Lockhart, C. (1994). *Reflective teaching in second language classrooms.* New York: Cambridge University Press.

Index

H

Humor, 90

I

Instructional Innovation and Improvement of Instruction Grants, 46
Instructors. *See* Teacher(s)
Invited lectures, 44

L

Lecture(s), 79–90
  brainstorming sessions, 87
  case method teaching, 87–88
  content area, 45–46
  delivering scripted, 75–77
  descriptive notes on, 47
  differences between speech styles of lecturers, 47
  discuss strengths and weaknesses as lecturer with students, 81–82
  expository lecturing, 86–87
  getting ready to, 88–90
  humor, 90
  importance and role of, 71
  invited, 44
  know material, 81–83
  lecture transcripts, 72–76
  live *versus* videotaped, 71–72, 74
  organizational plan, 85–86
  plan for short periods of time, 82
  publisher's lectures, 72–76
  reports on public, 45
  role play, 87
  set realistic expectations about lecture, 82–83
  Socratic methods, 87
  structured reviewing, 76–77
  structure in three phases, 83
  teach students to interact with lecturers, 34–35
  topics for delivering original lectures, 83–86
  video-recorded, 44, 71–74
  video recordings to illustrate characteristics of, 46–47
  whole-class, 34, 44, 87, 91–100
  See also Mini-lectures
Lecture transcripts, 72–76

Library report, 45
Listening-to-learn, 19–20, 143

M

Magnets, 22
Mini-lectures, 68–78
  delivering scripted, 75–77
  explain before beginning lecture, 77–78
  live to class, 71–72
  role of substantive content in course, 69–71
  speaking from outline or list of talking points, 75
  topics for, related to class size and configuration, 102
  visual supports, 75
  words of caution, 74
  working with publisher's lectures and lecture transcripts, 72–74
  See also Lecture(s)

N

Names, learn student, 24–27
  ask students to help, 25
  "first letter only" rule, 27
  use index cards as flash cards, 26
  videotape members of class, 26
Native English speakers (NES), 49–66
  attention span of, 86
  interacting with classmates, 60–66
    arrange for NES speakers to visit class, 61–62
    invited former NES students to visit class, 65–66
    small-group discussions with NES college students, 65
    student surveys of opinions of matriculated NES students, 62–65
  interacting with instructors, 50–59
    importance of student relationships with, 51–52, 54
    mainstream settings, 58–59
    student interaction with, 50–59
Netiquette rules, 138–139
Note taking
  during lectures, 47
  observing speaking-to-learn behaviors, 58
Numeric conventions for analyzing stress patterns, 124–127